still not good

by
sharon kapitula

This book is a work of fiction. Characters, places, and incidents are the product of the author's imagination. Any resemblance to actual persons, living or dead, events, or locales is coincidental.

ISBN: 978-1-7368316-0-1

I've sat on this text for a year due to the mixed reactions from friends who read the proof copy, but I decided to finally publish because my fictive reality may be relatable for others facing internal turmoil.

Warning you now, this story doesn't have a "happy" ending. That doesn't mean it won't eventually be different; mental health is fluid. Like an impressionist painting, this work aims to capture a snapshot of human experience during a moment in time.

I want to deeply thank everyone who has been supportive of me over the past few years; it's easy to underestimate the impact of small kindnesses. A special shoutout to Diana who kept me drawing when my capricious disposition kicked in and to Victoria who reminded me how rad it is to see my art in an official printed format <3

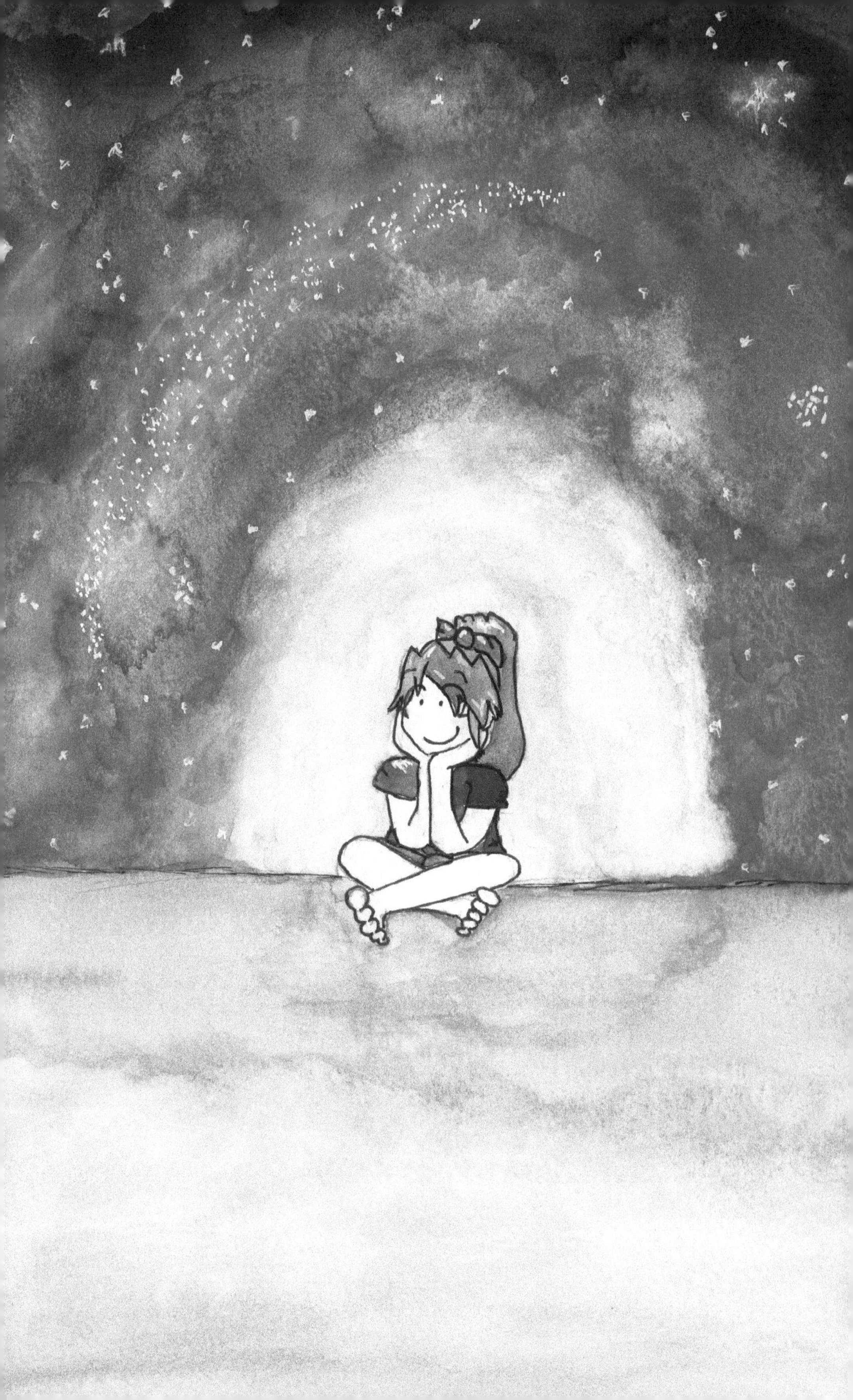

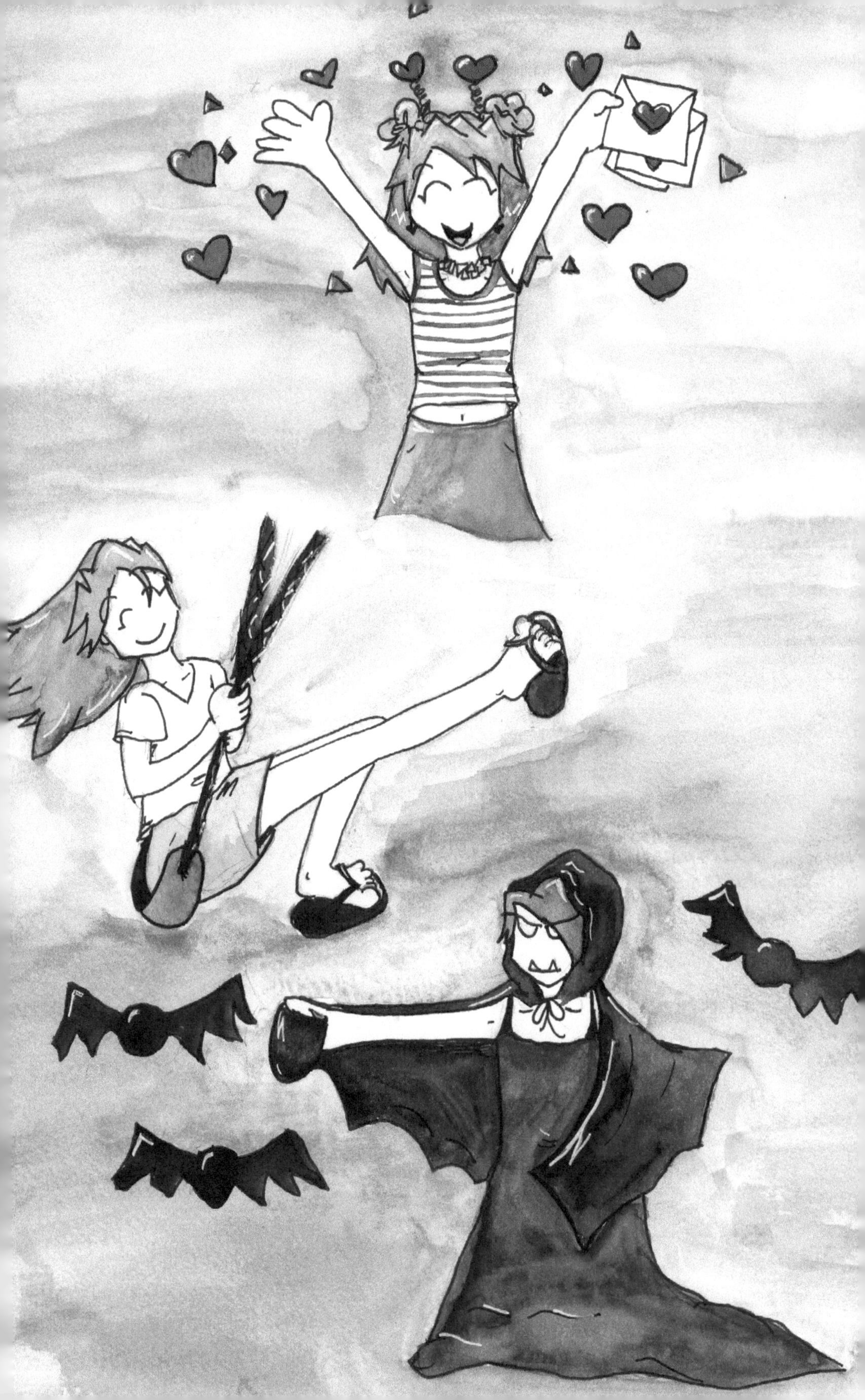

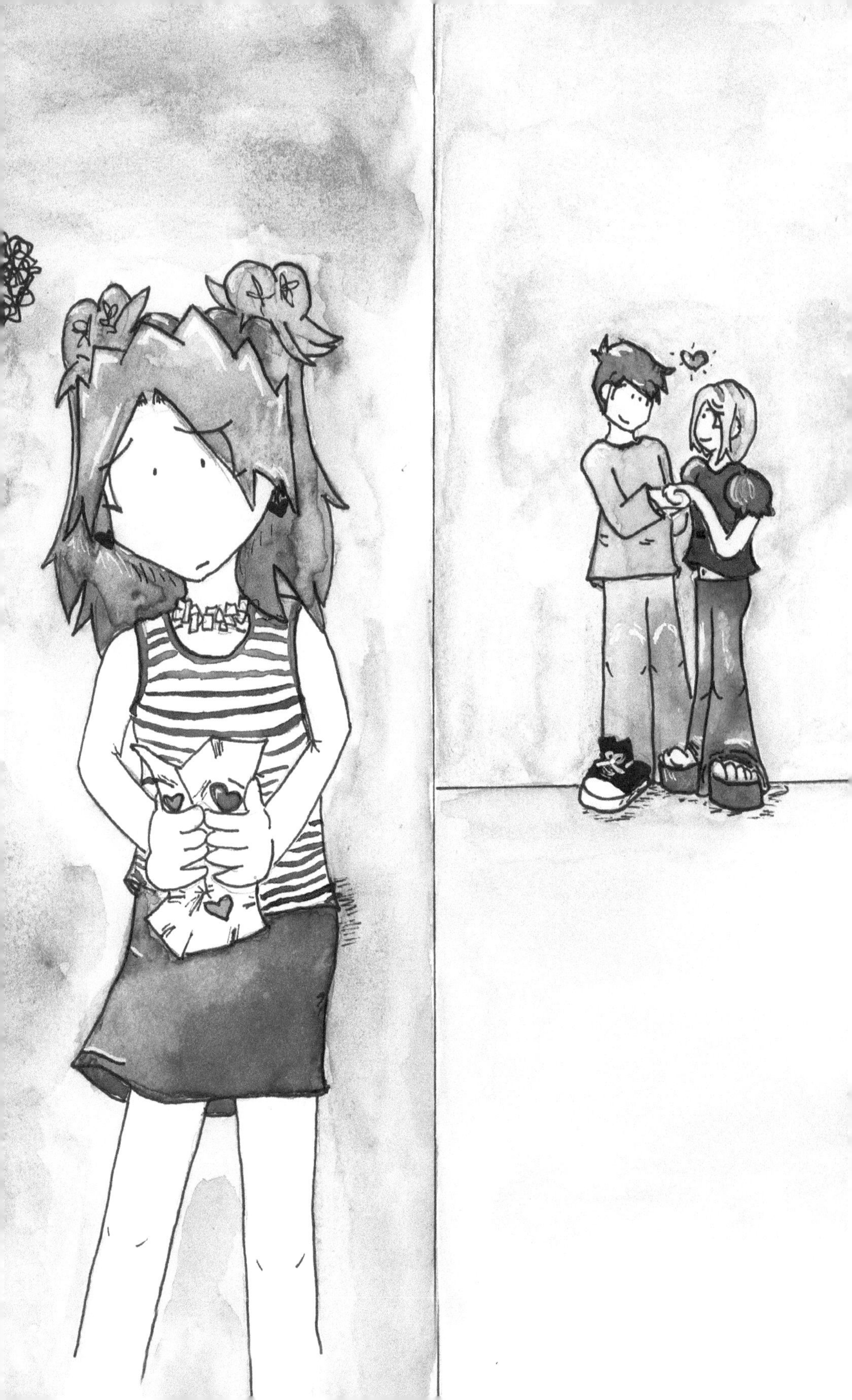

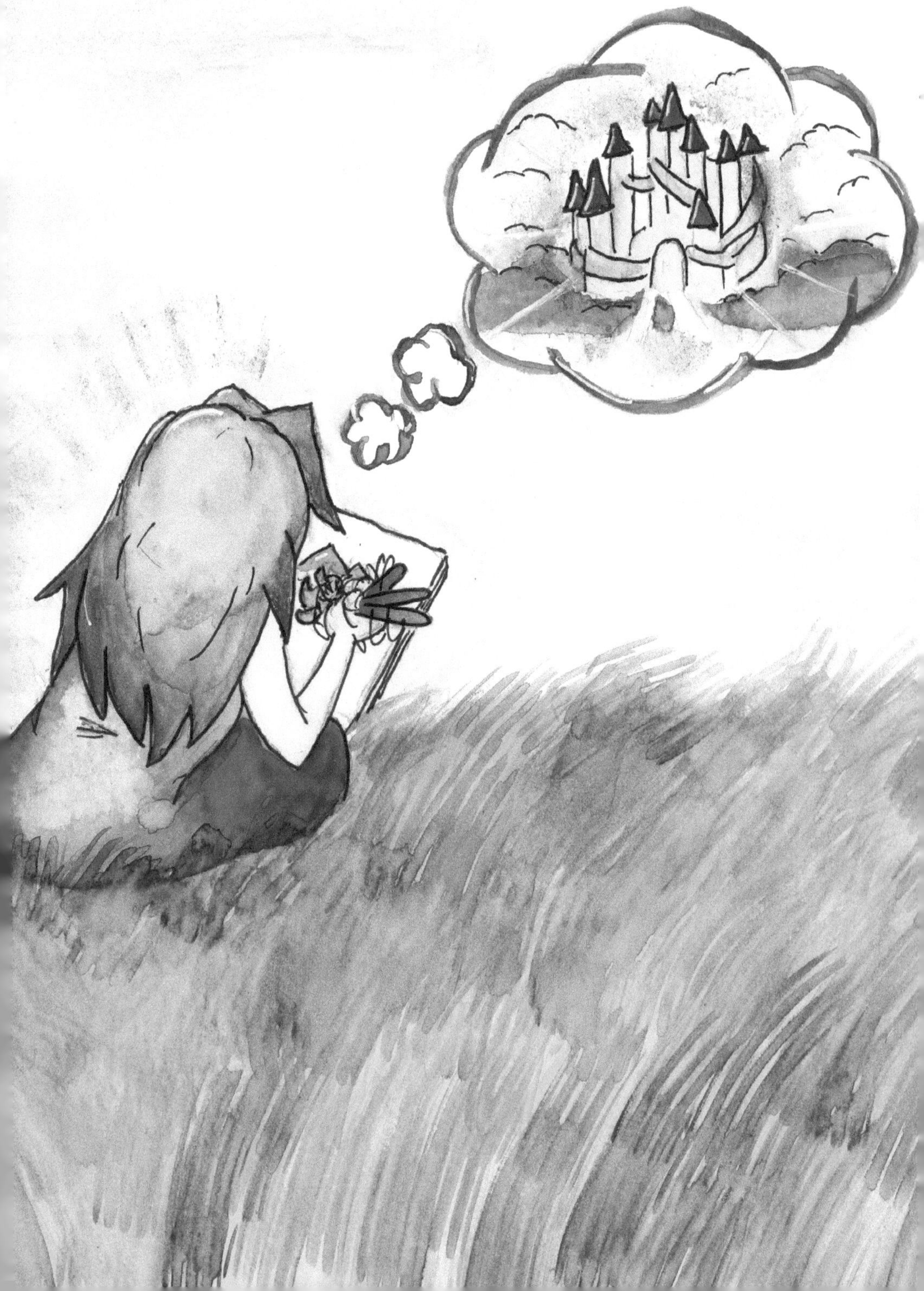

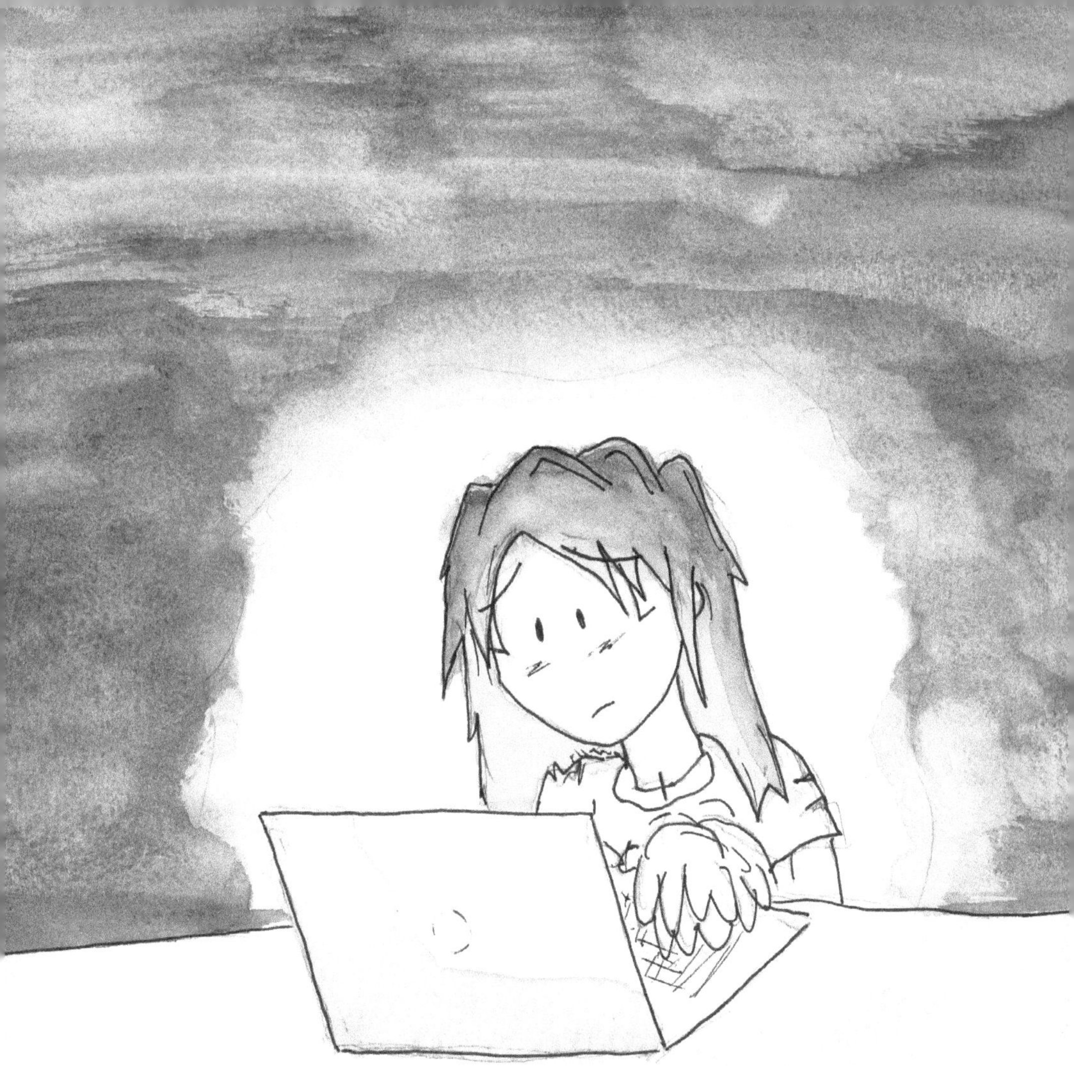

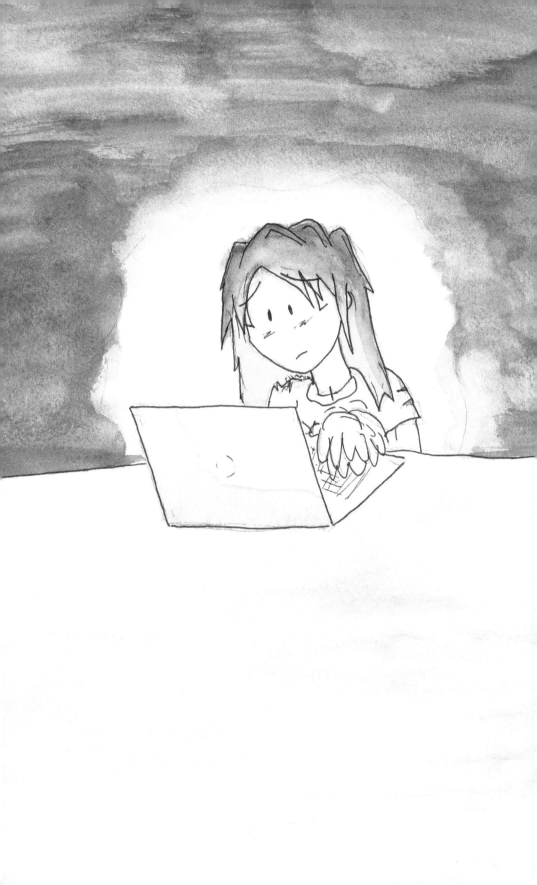

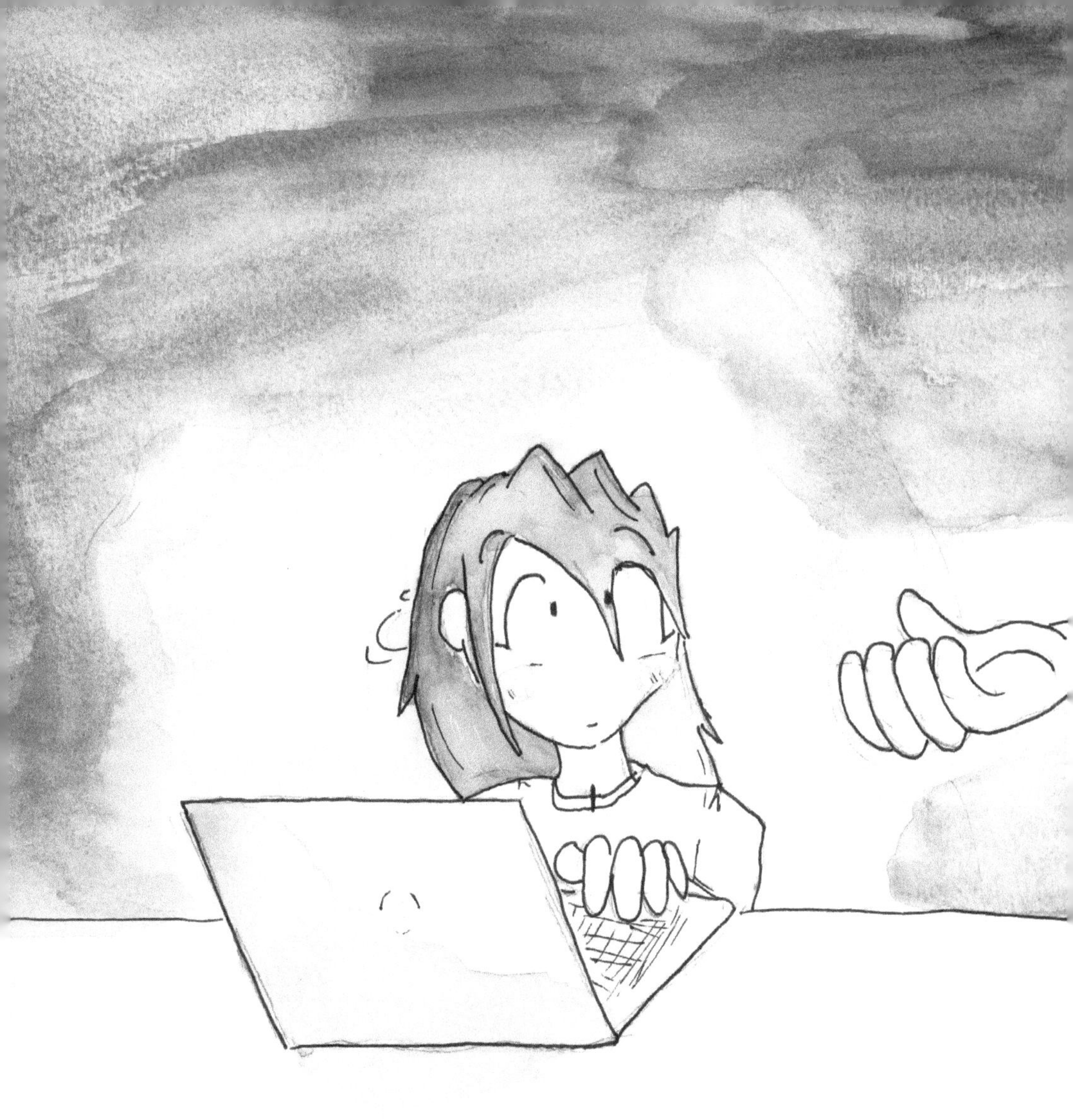

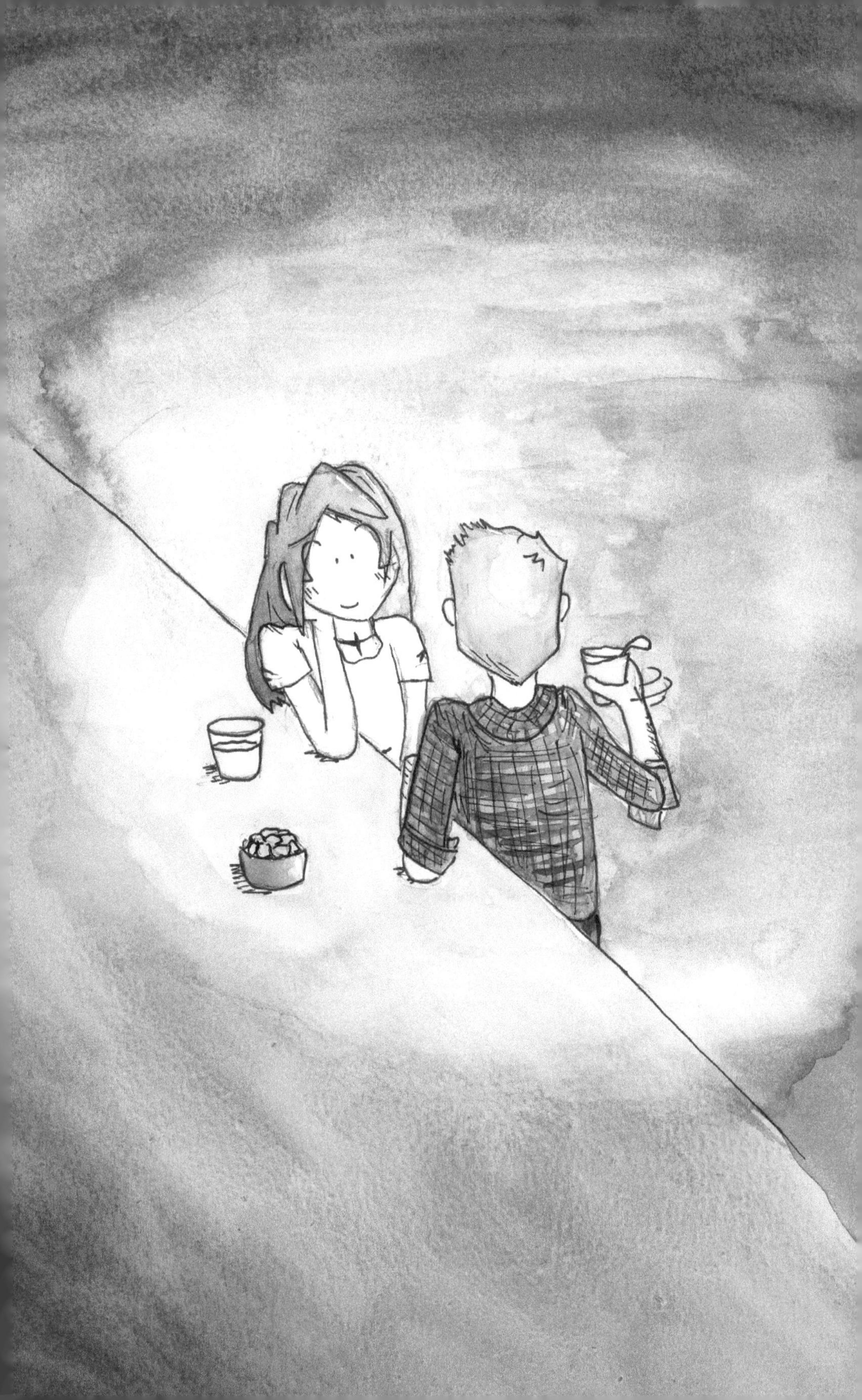

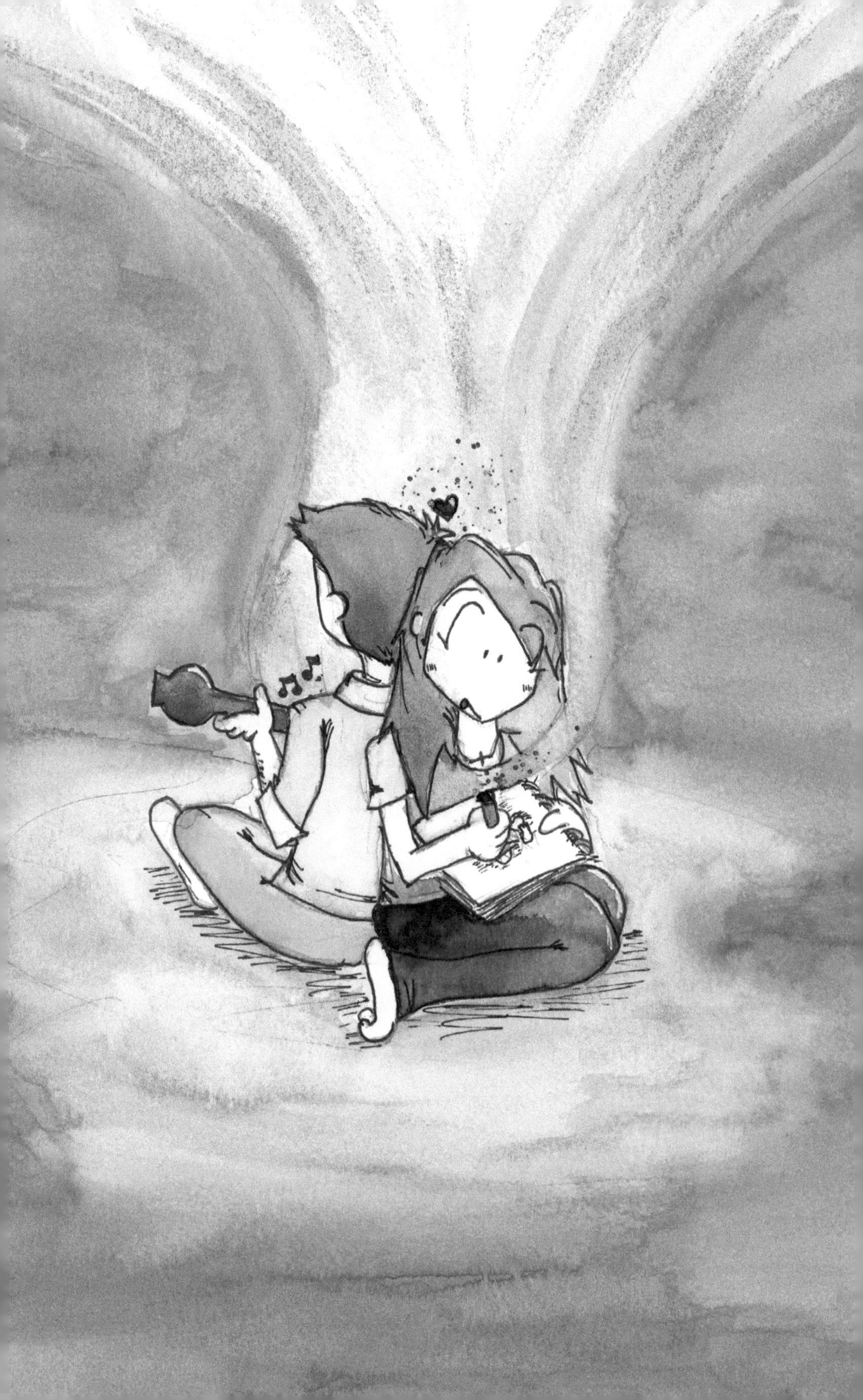

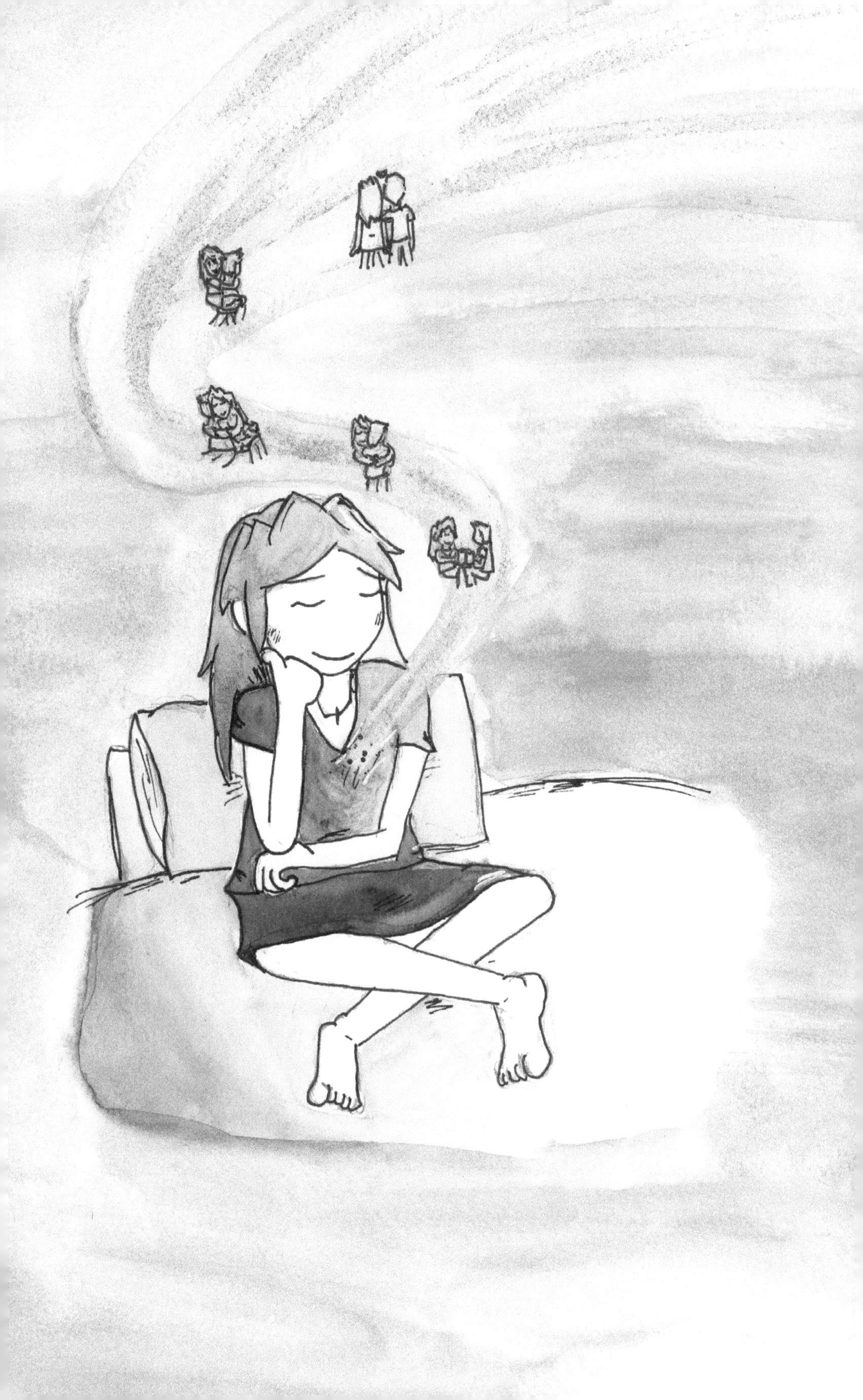

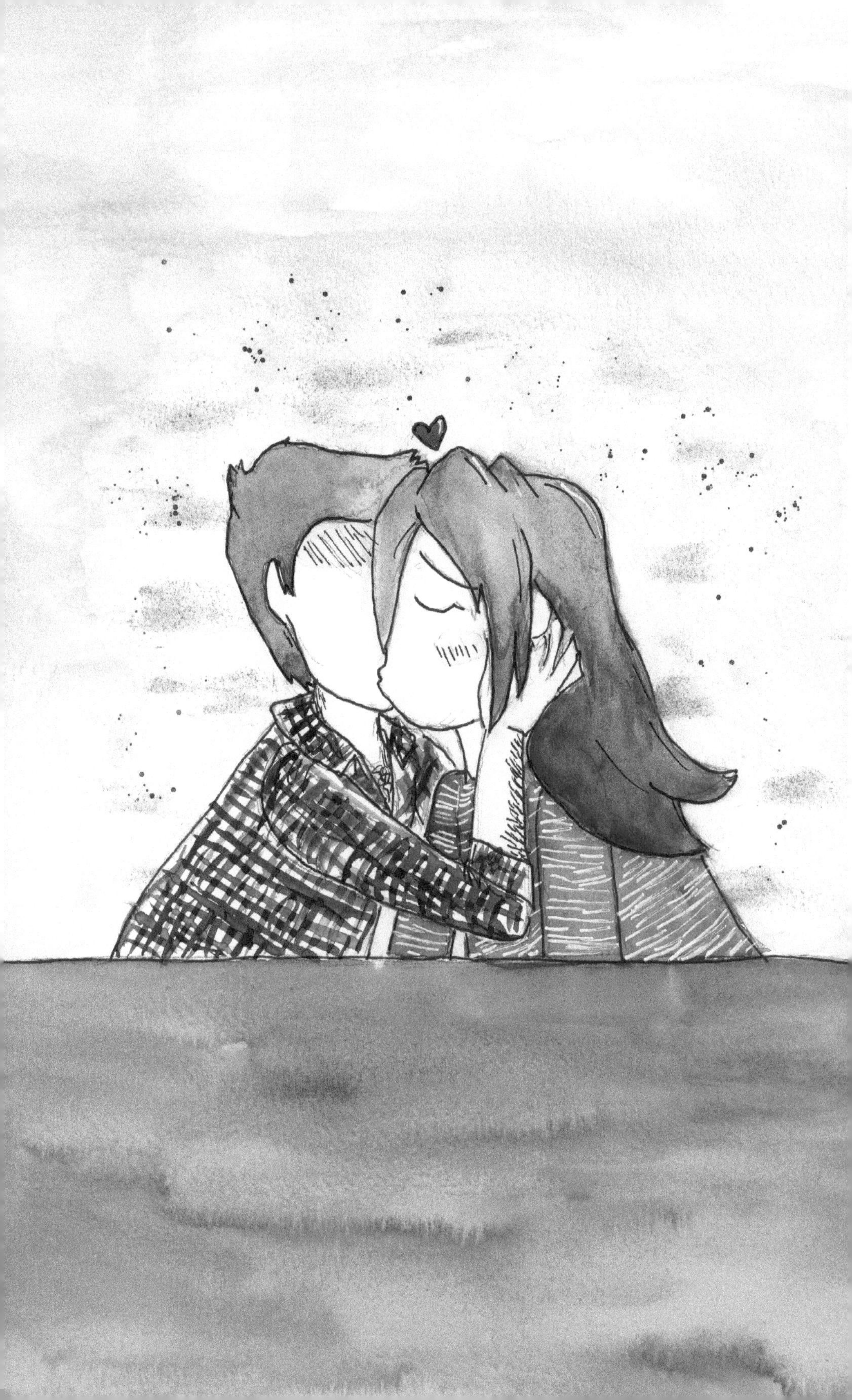

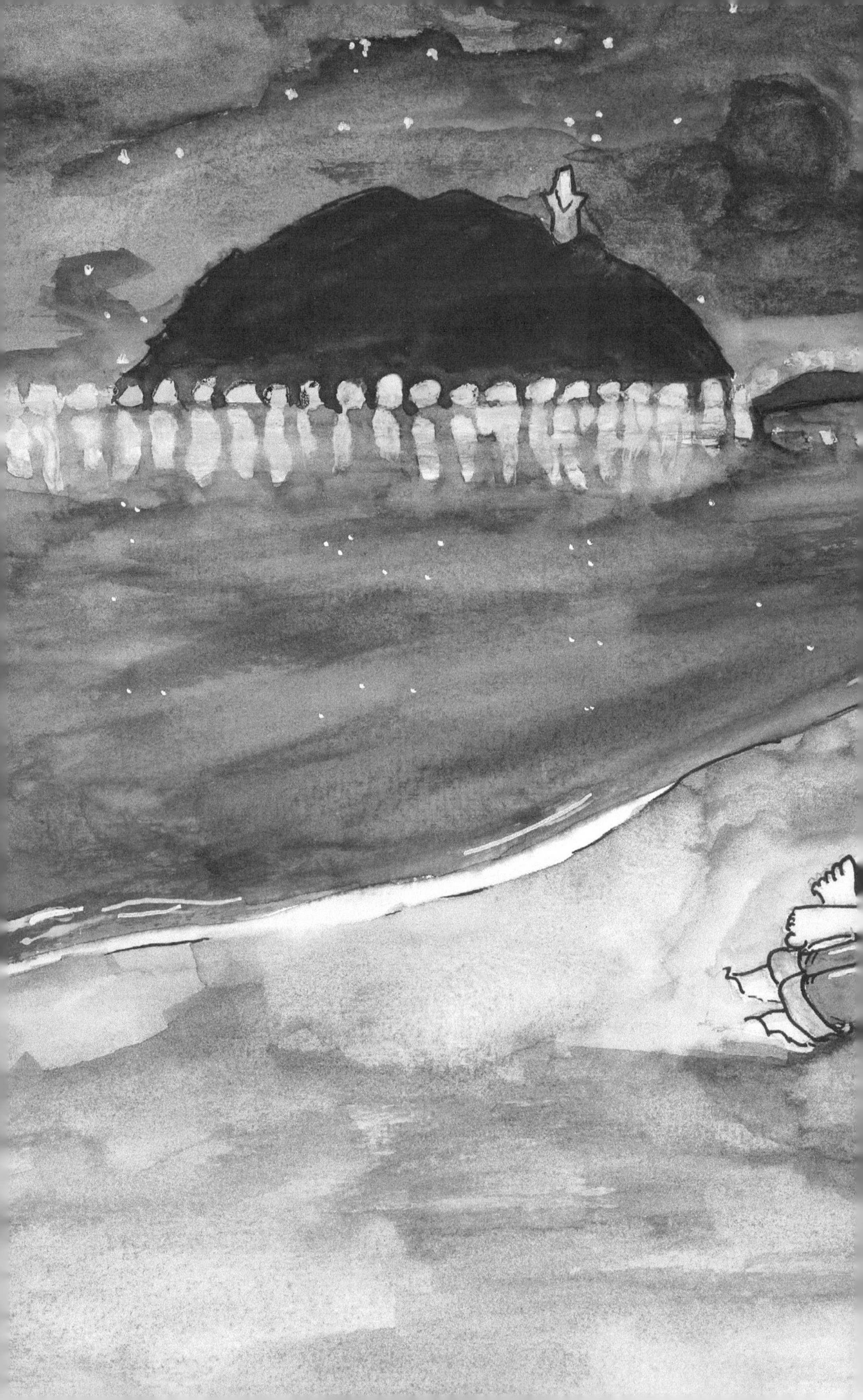

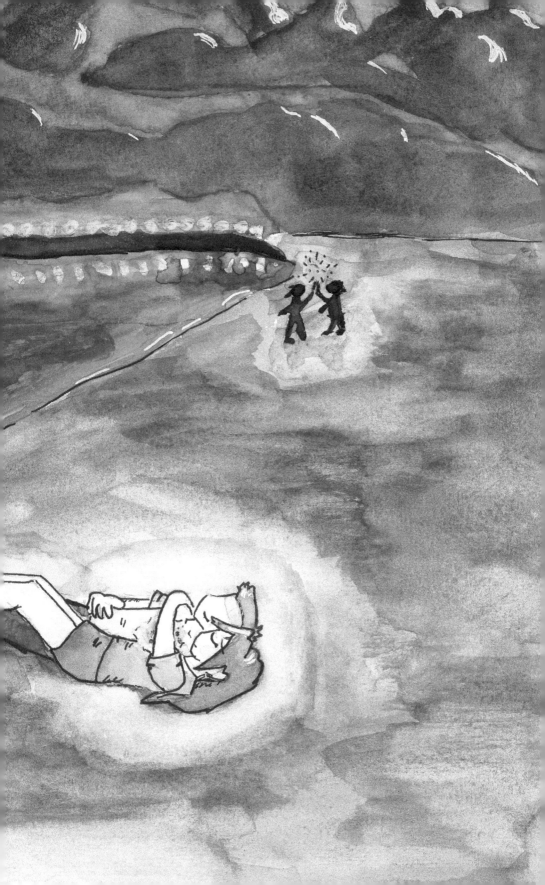

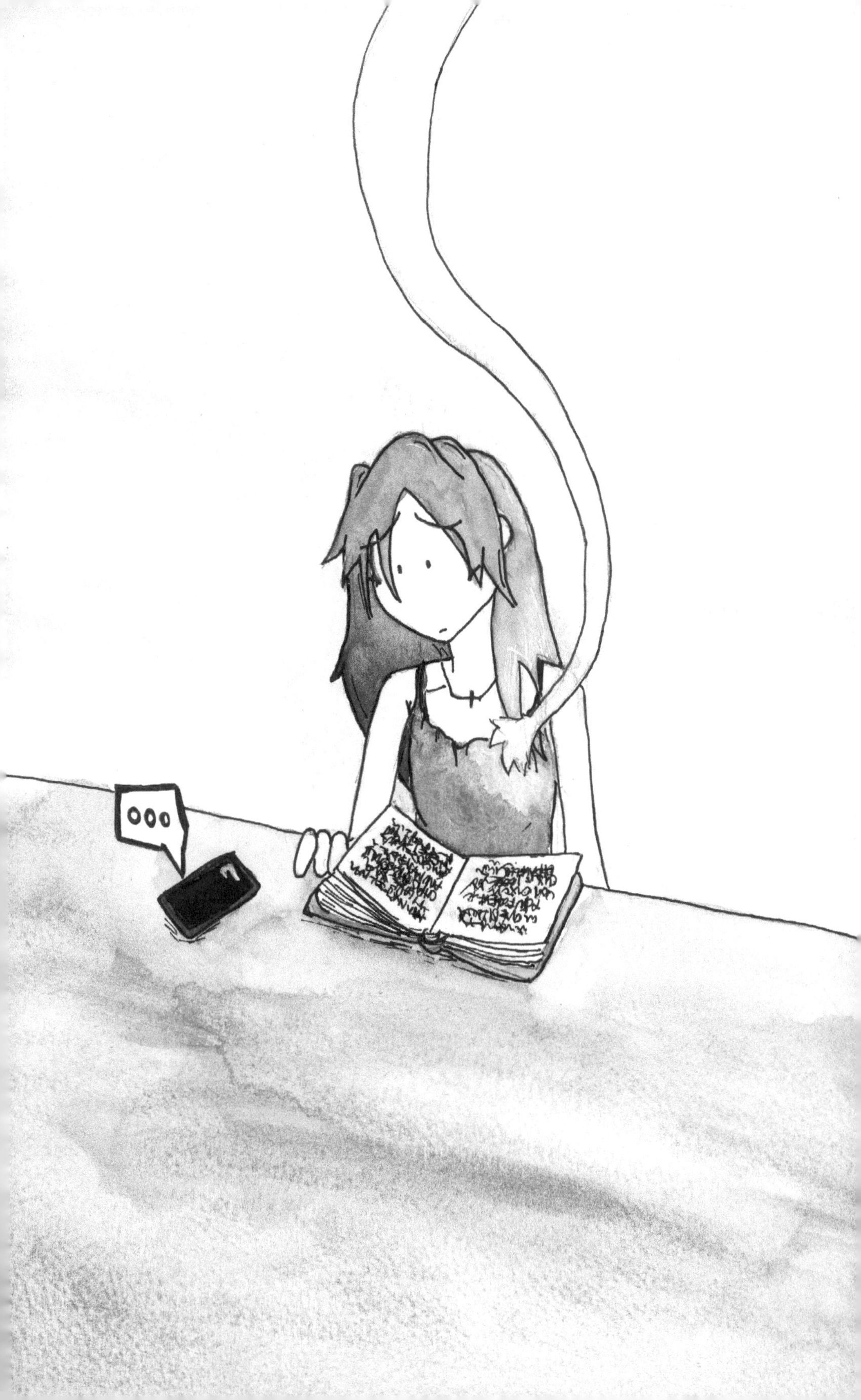

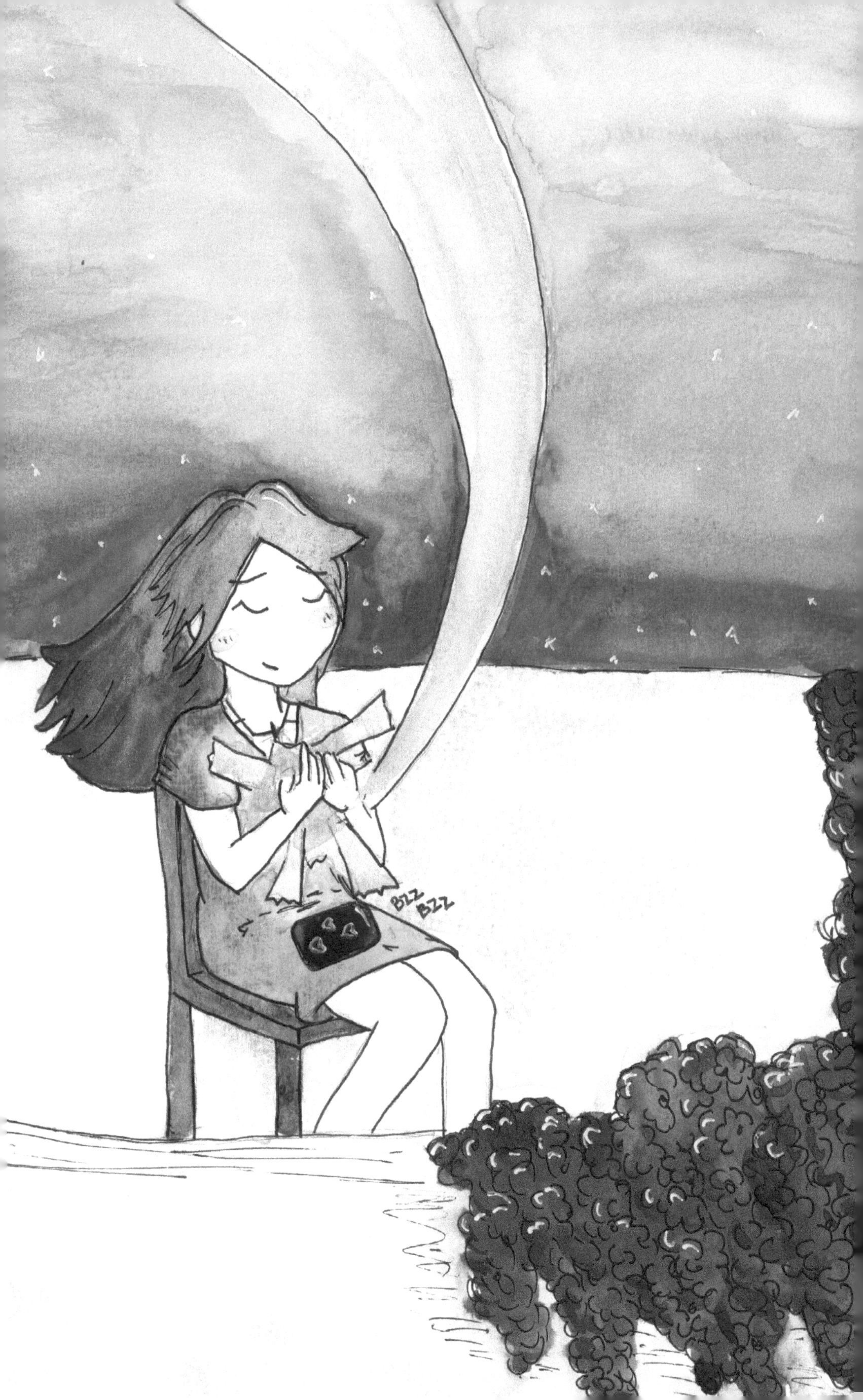
BZZ
BZZ

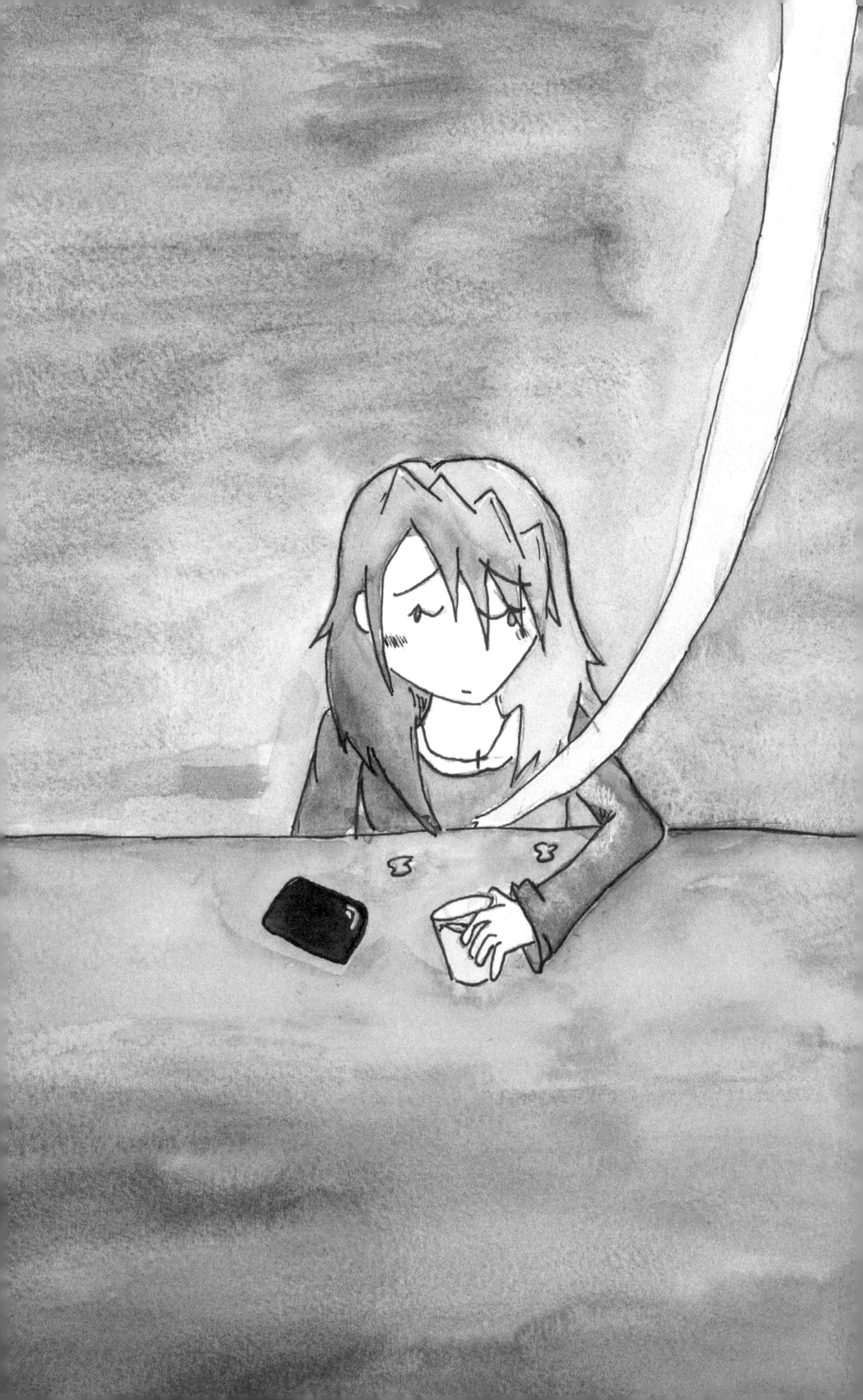

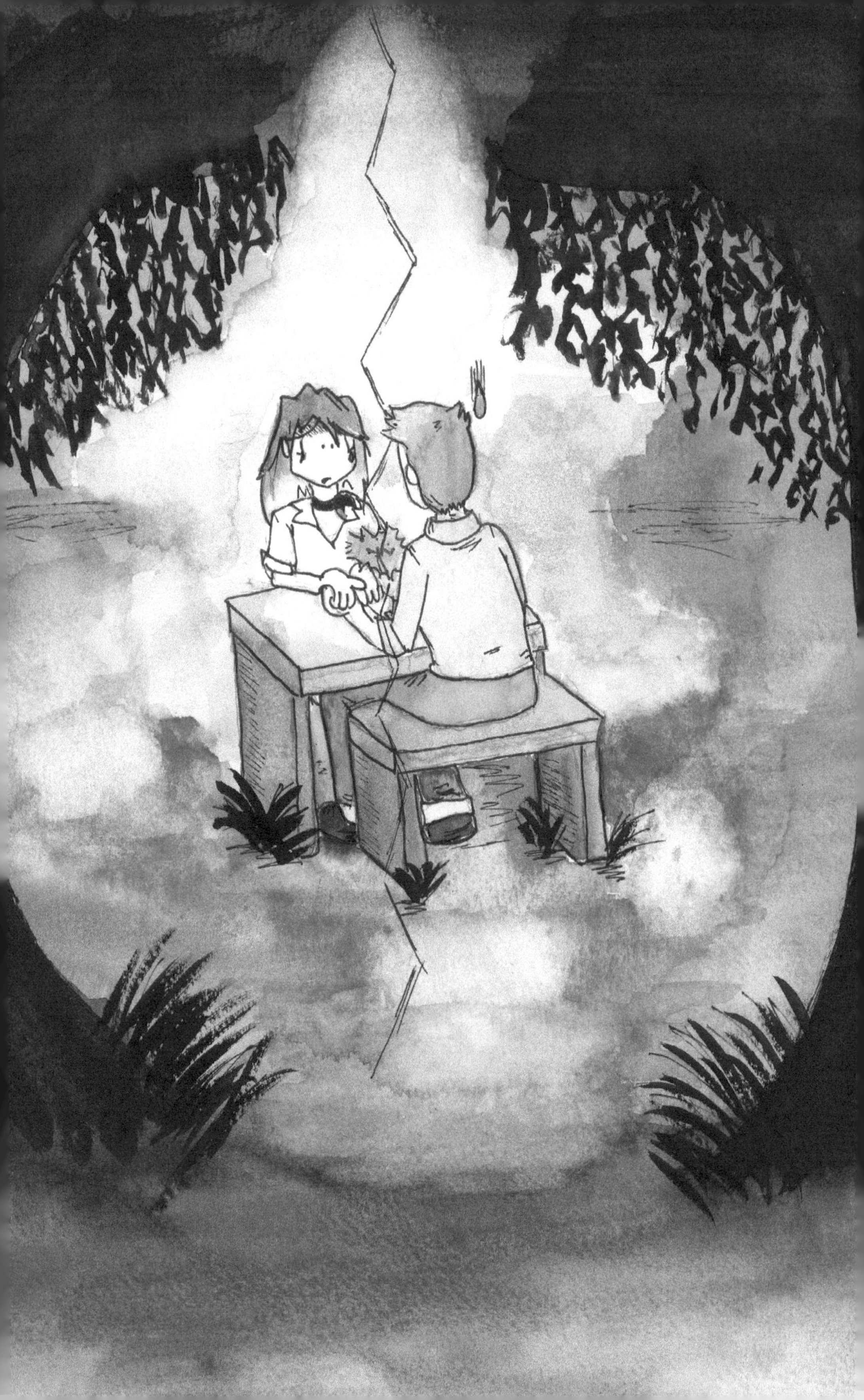

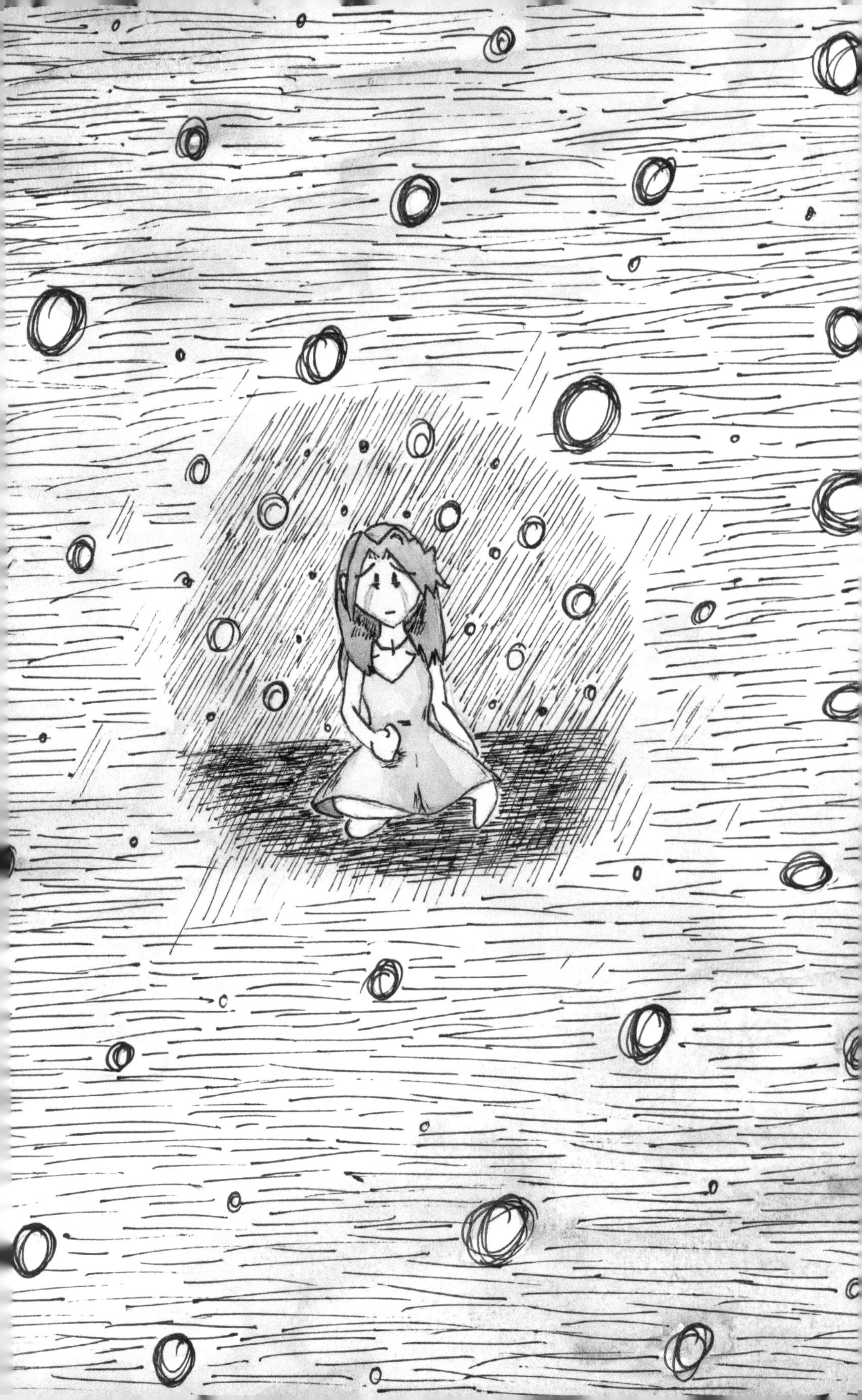

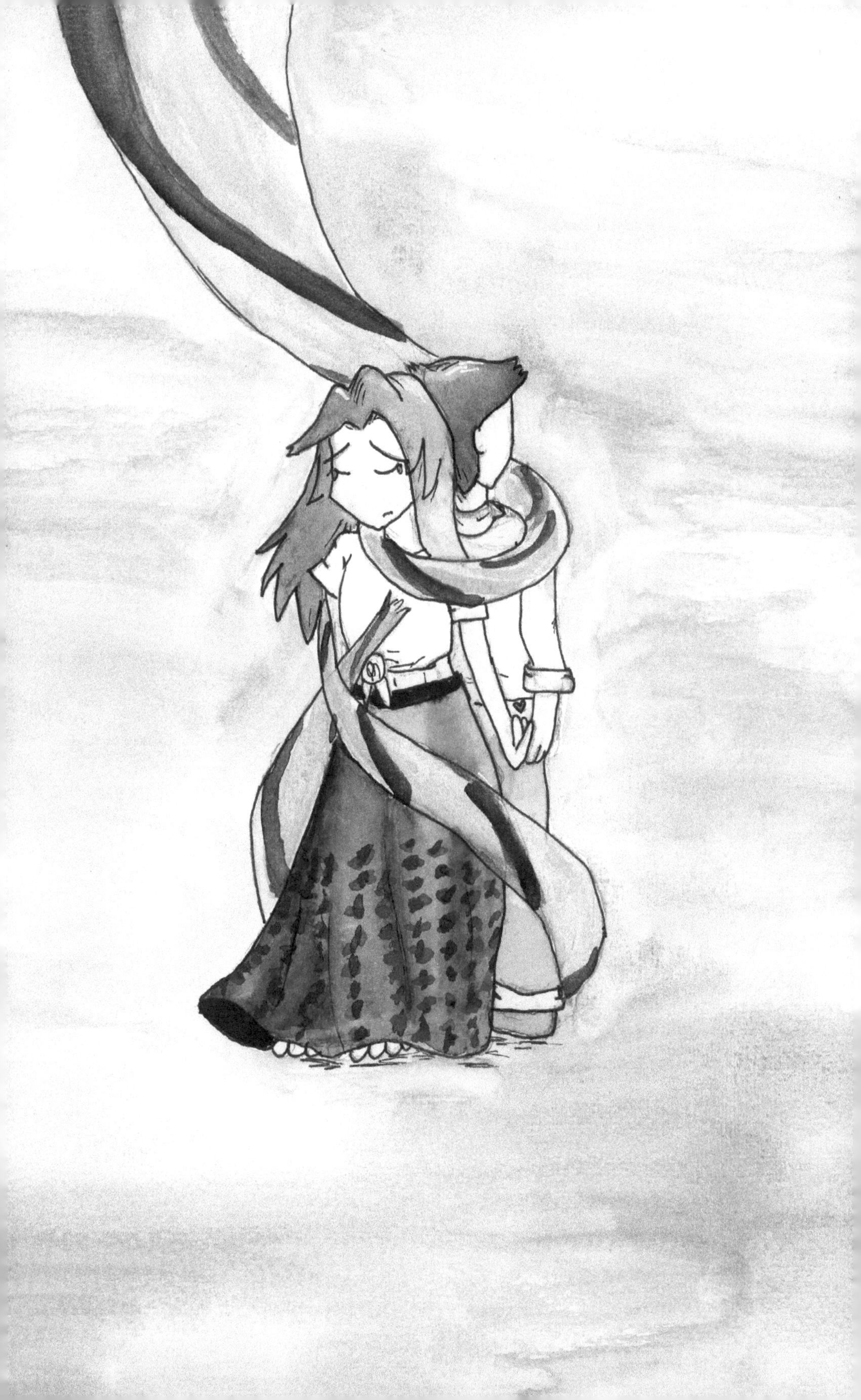

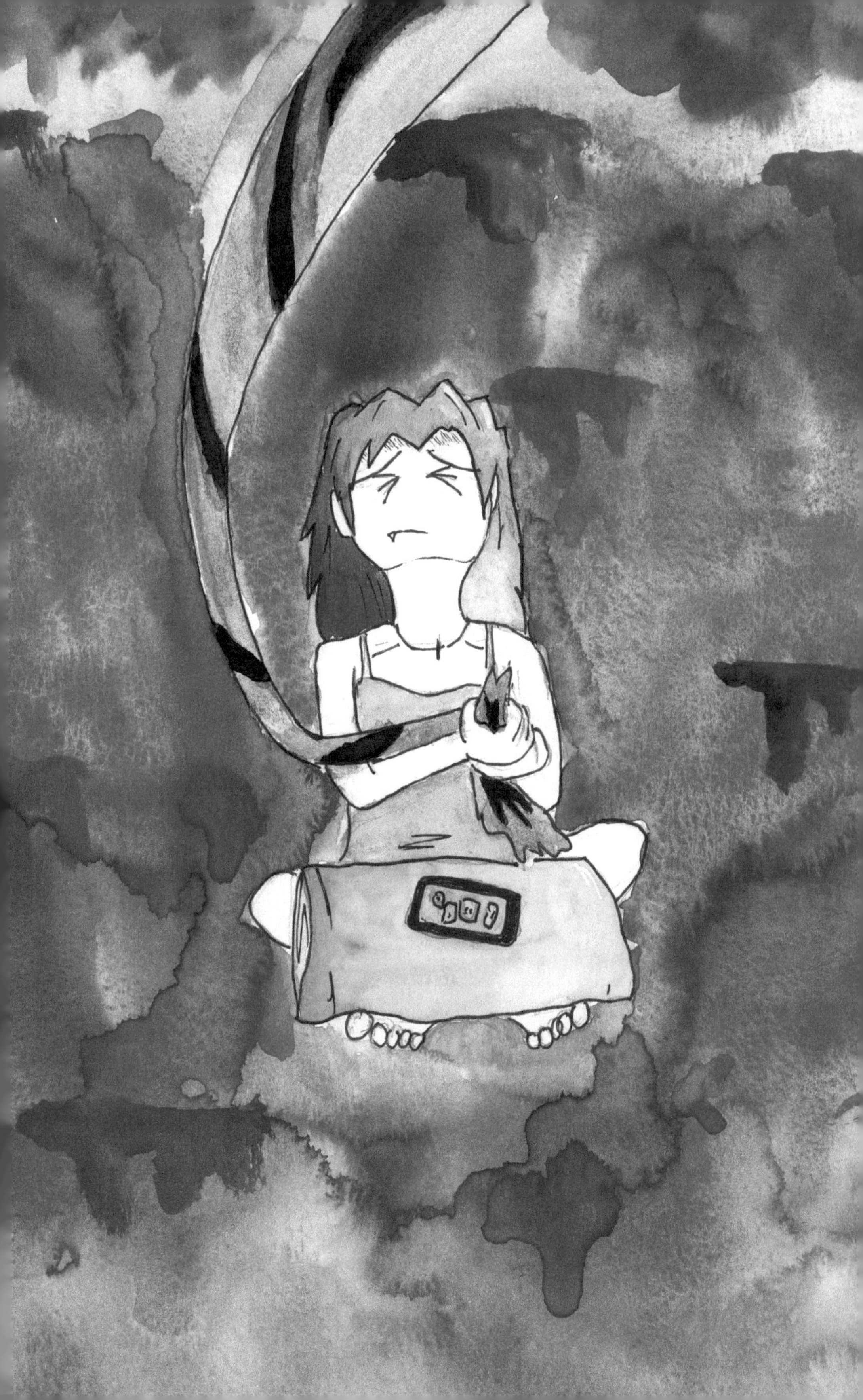

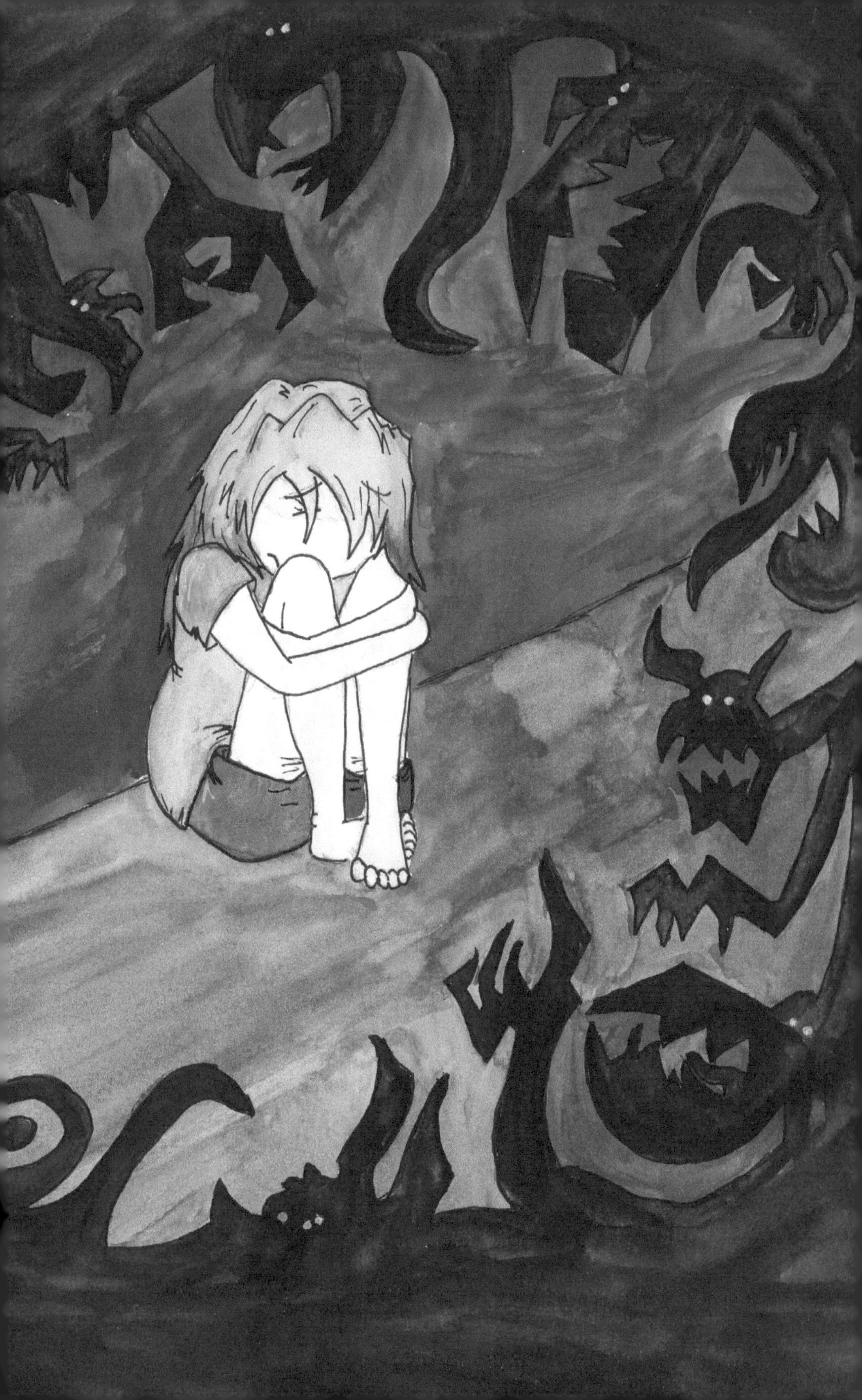

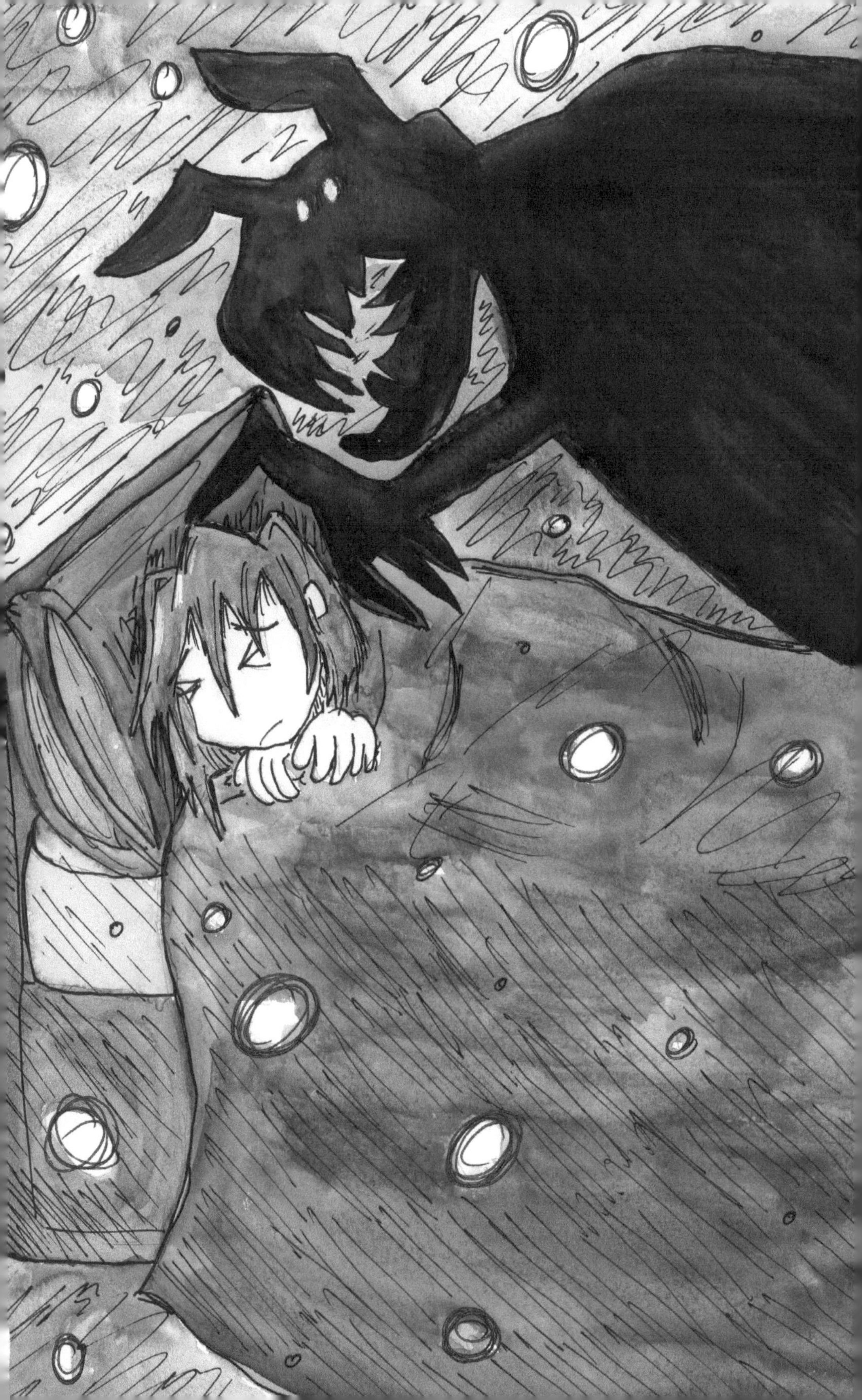

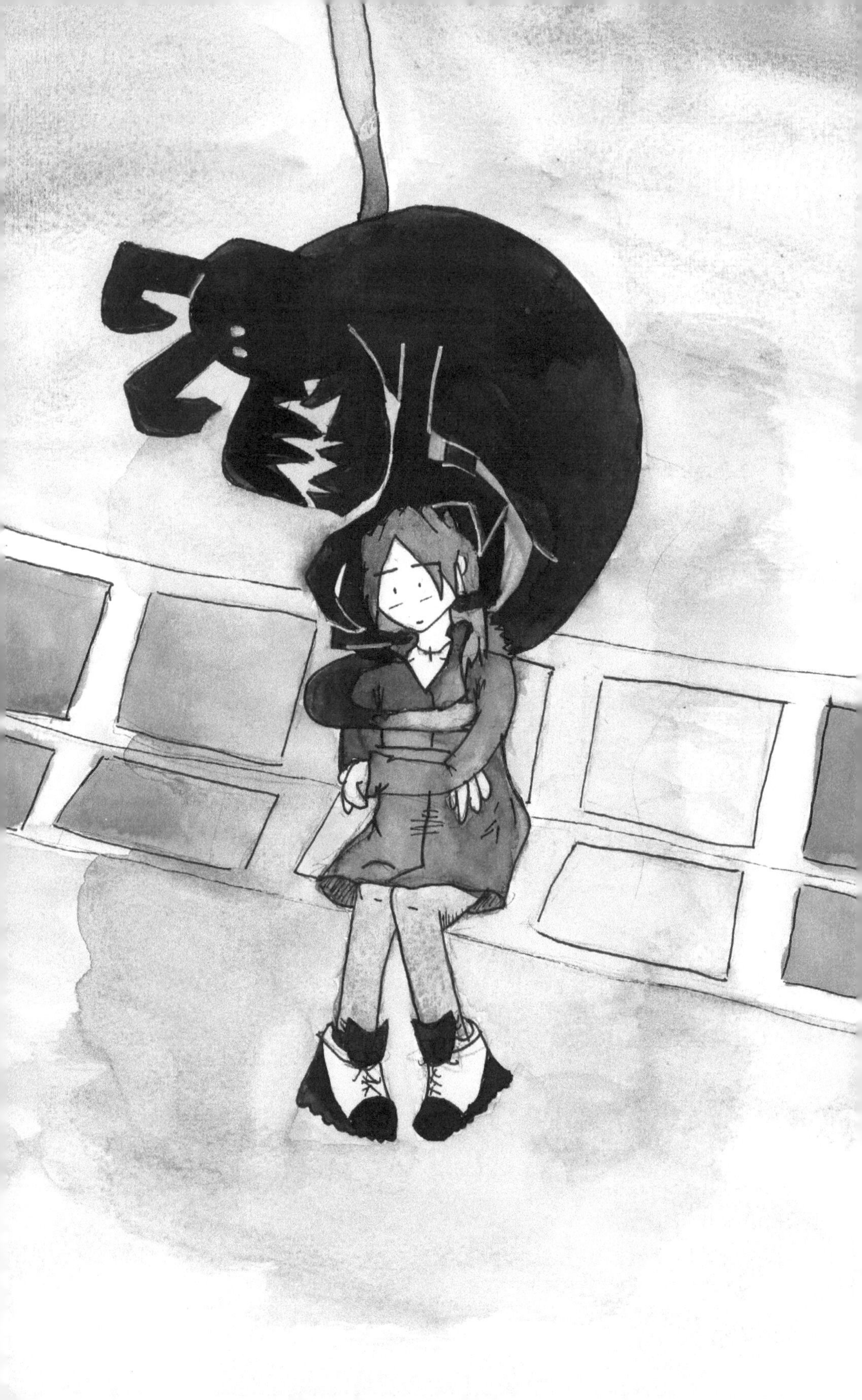

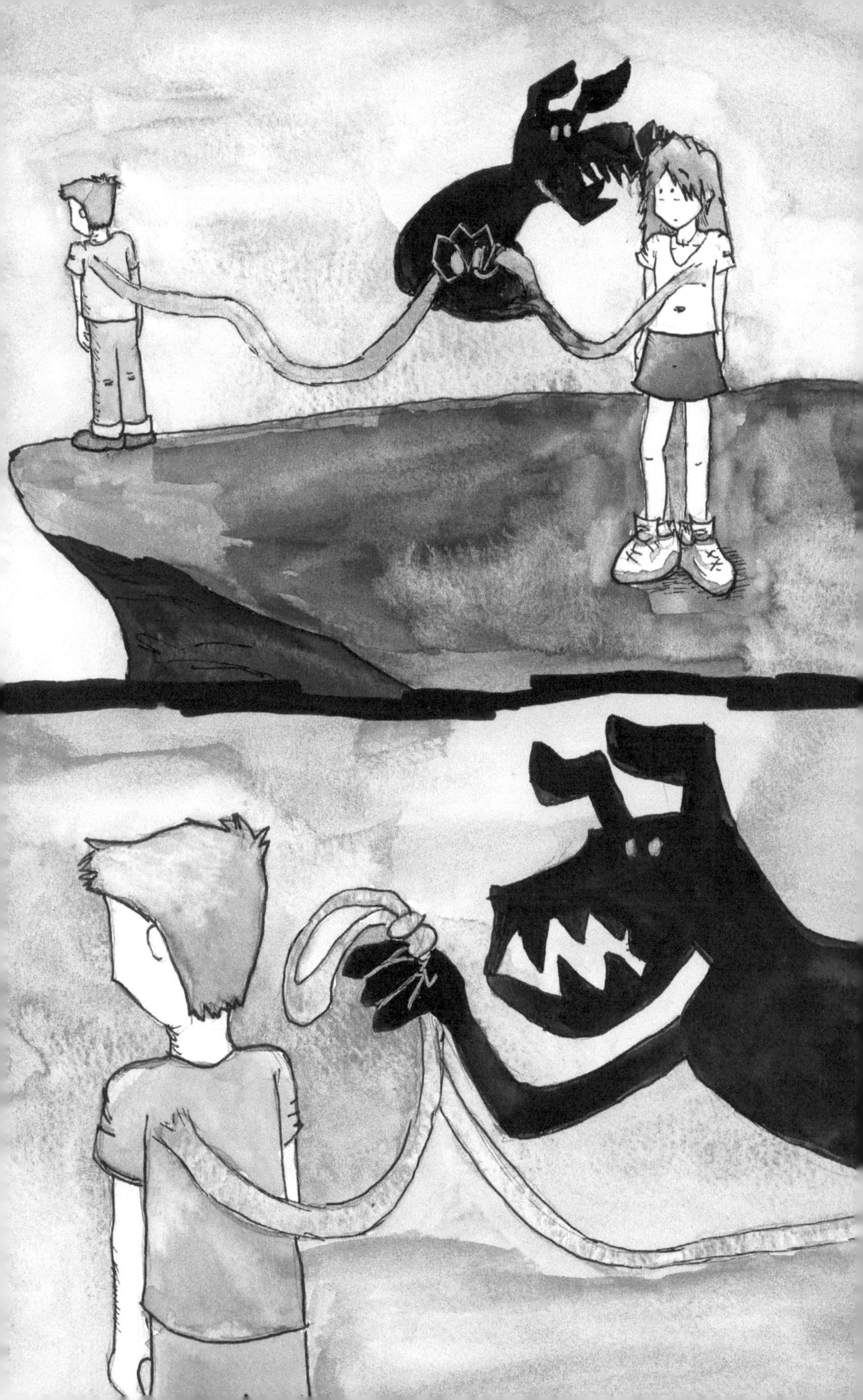

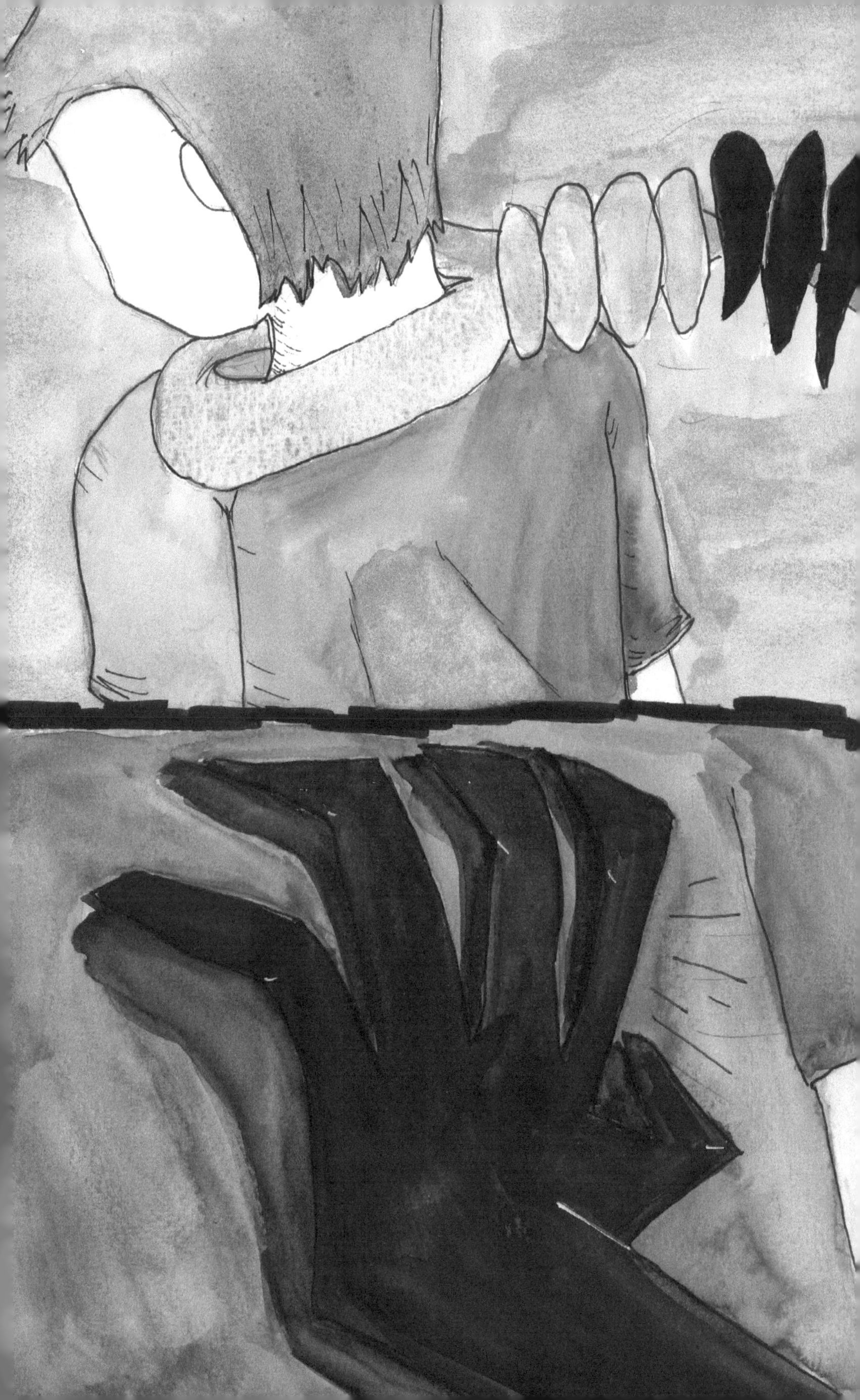

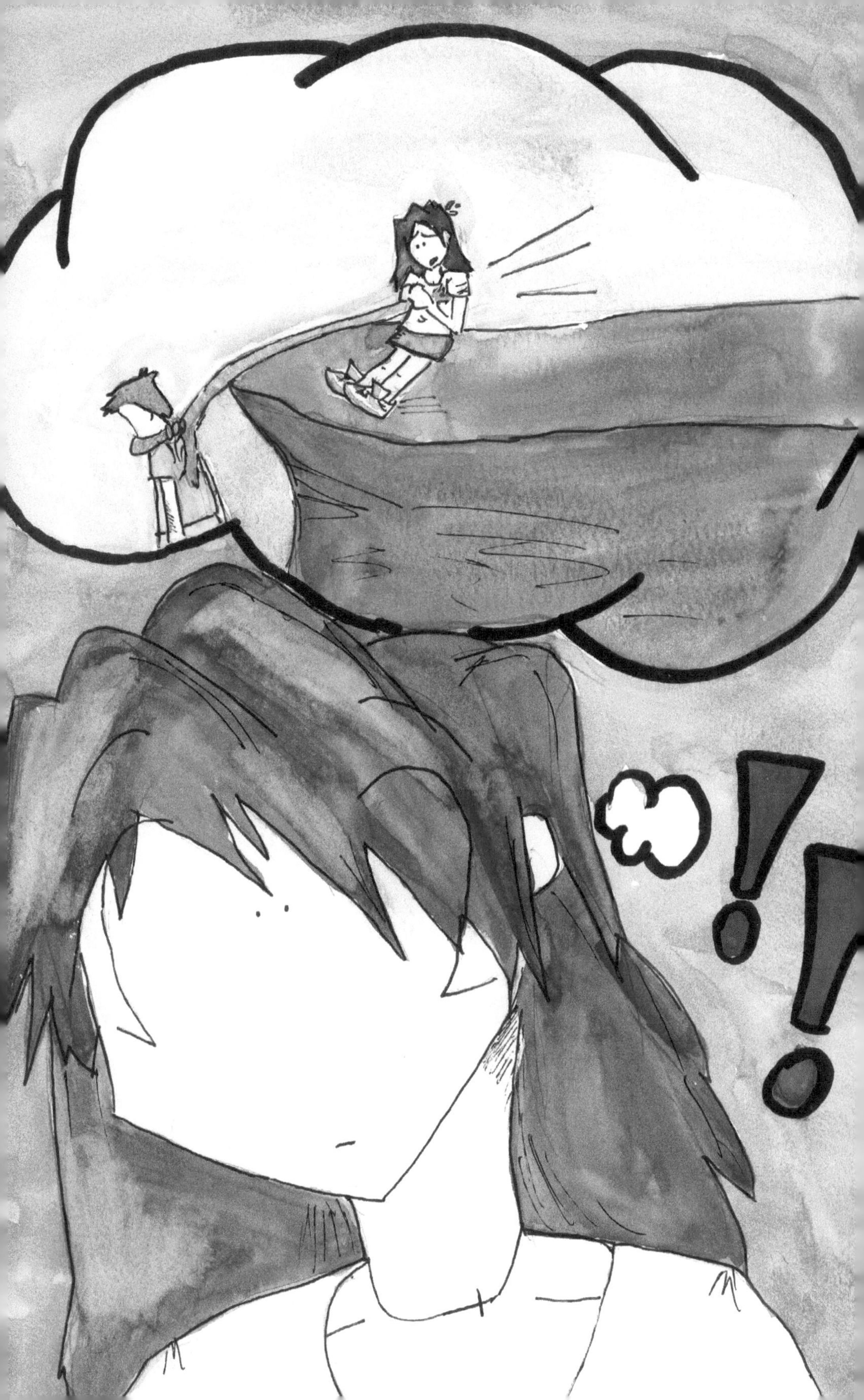

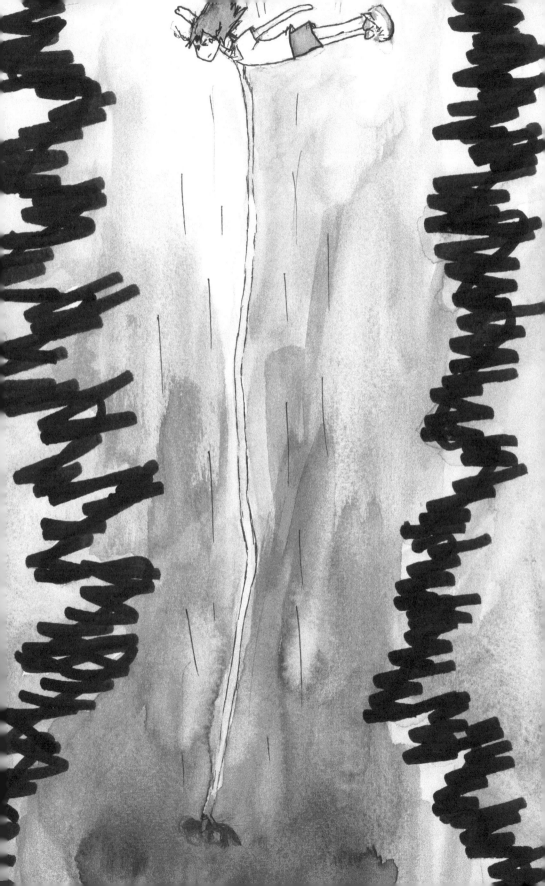

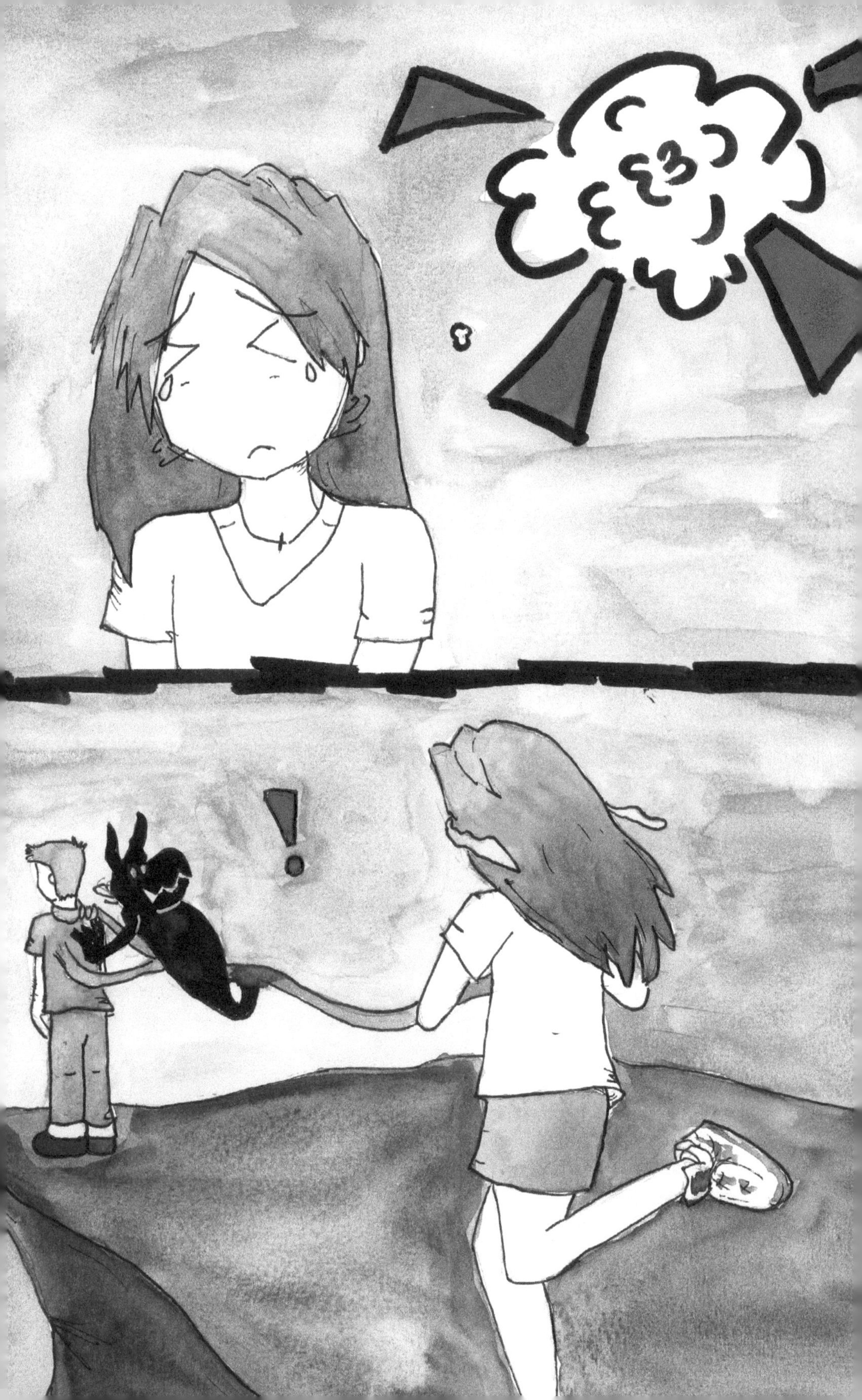

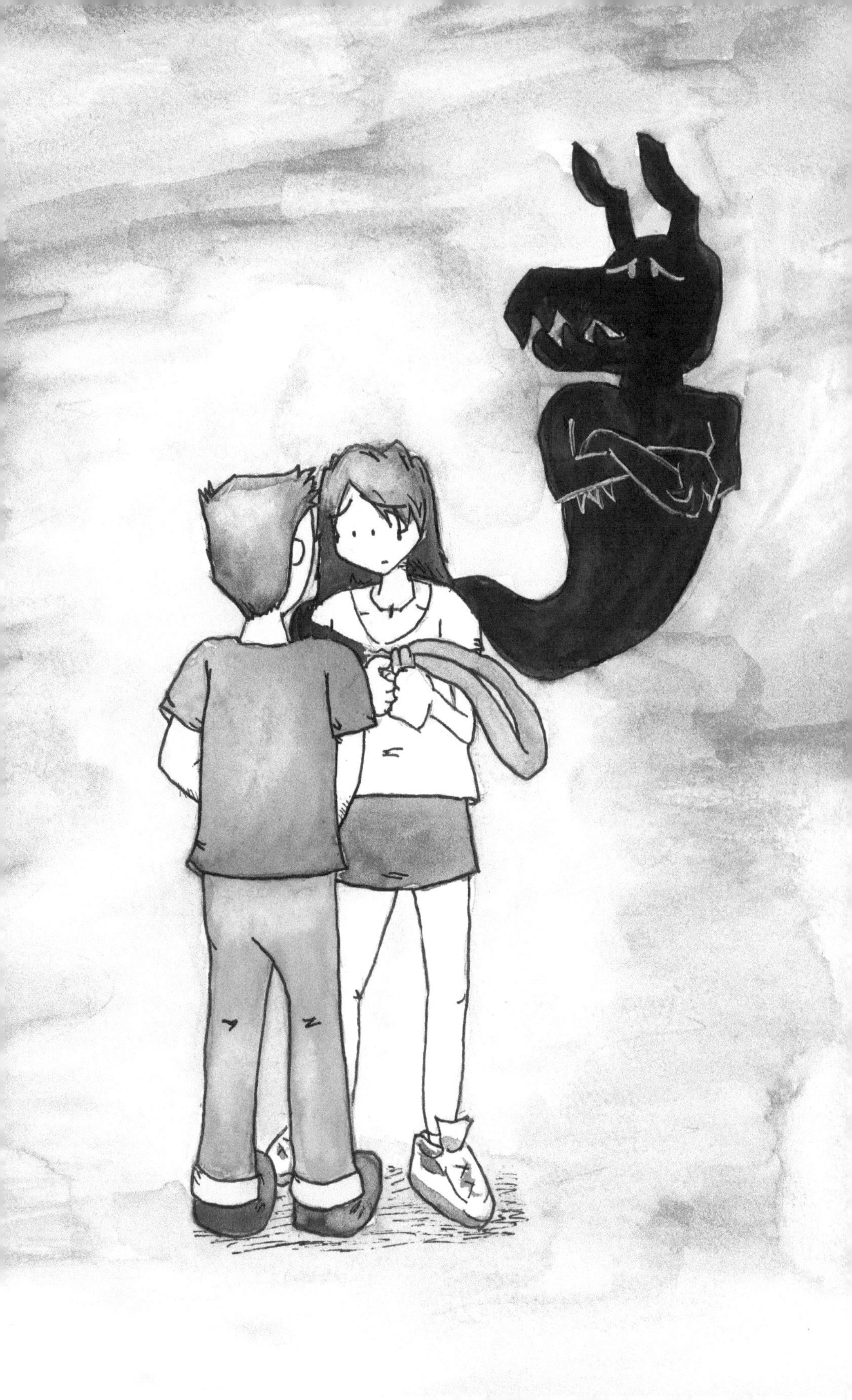

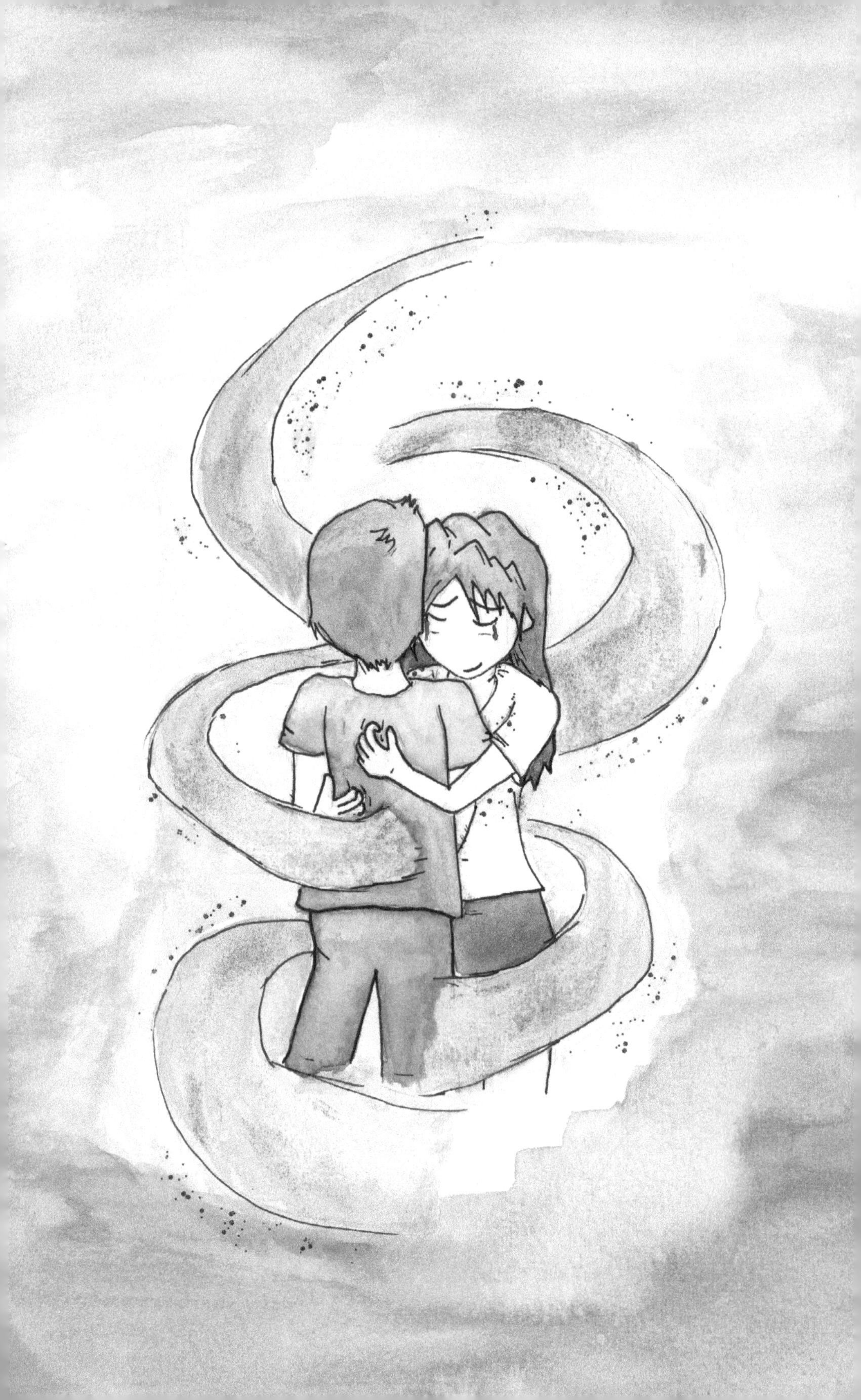

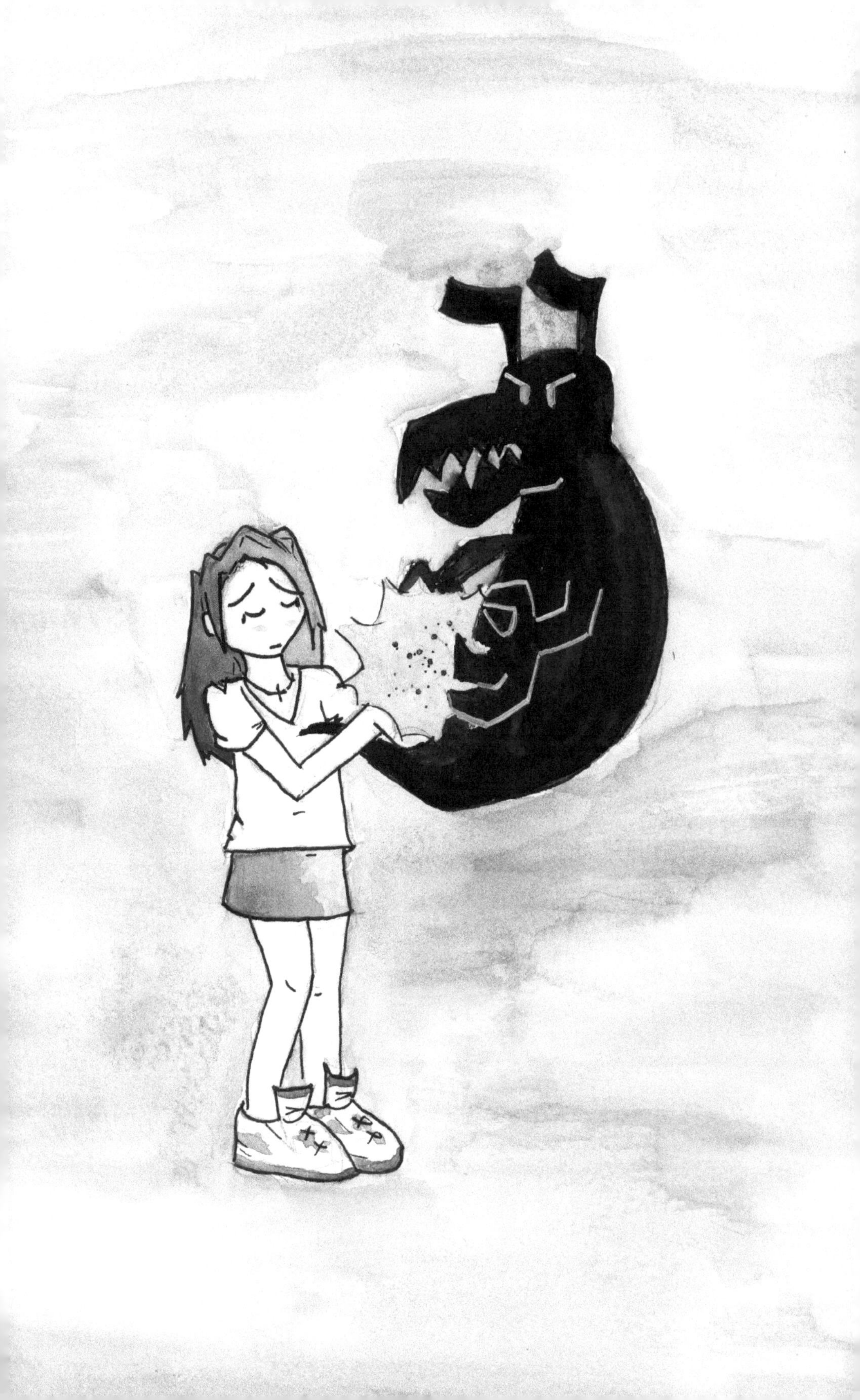

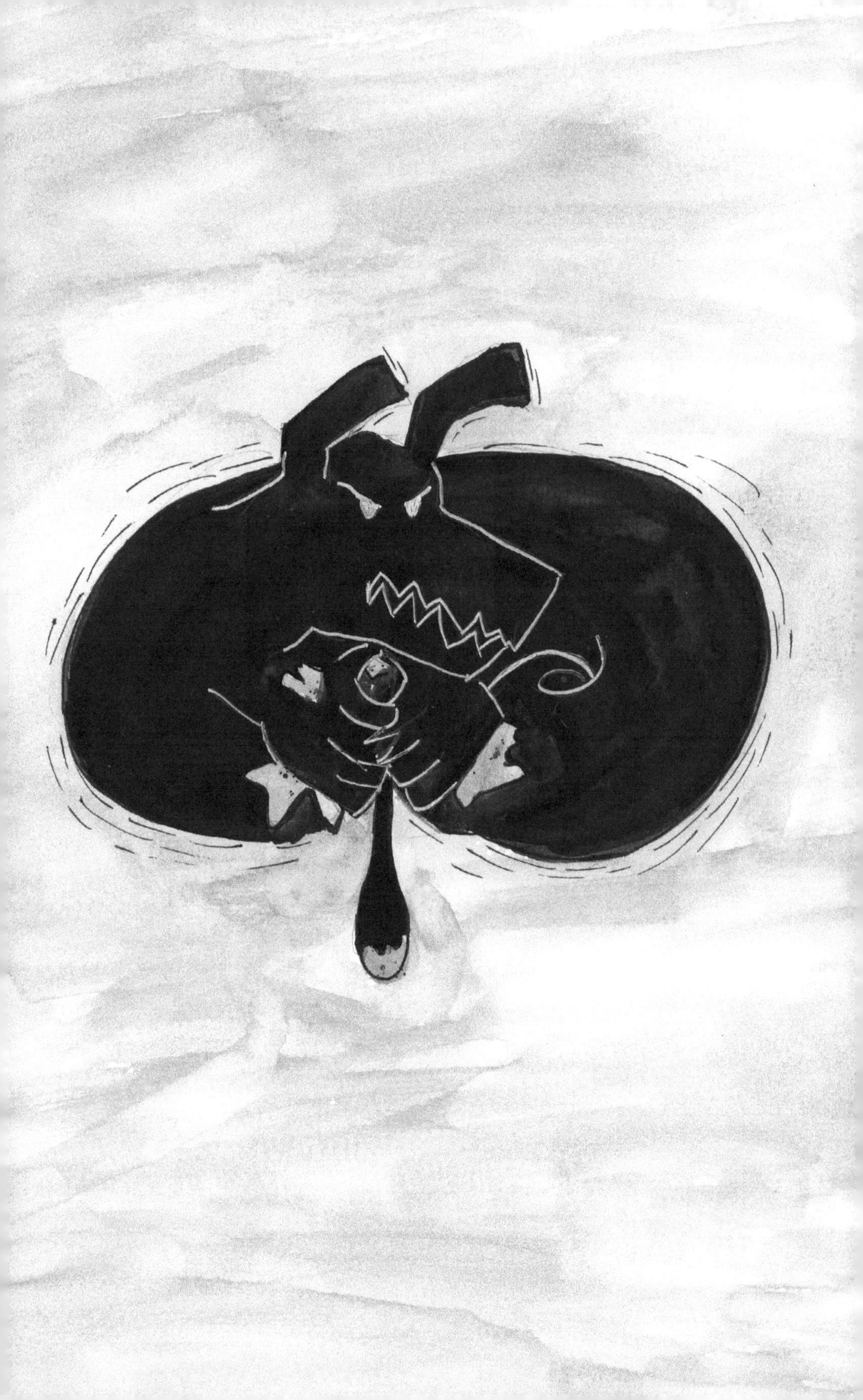

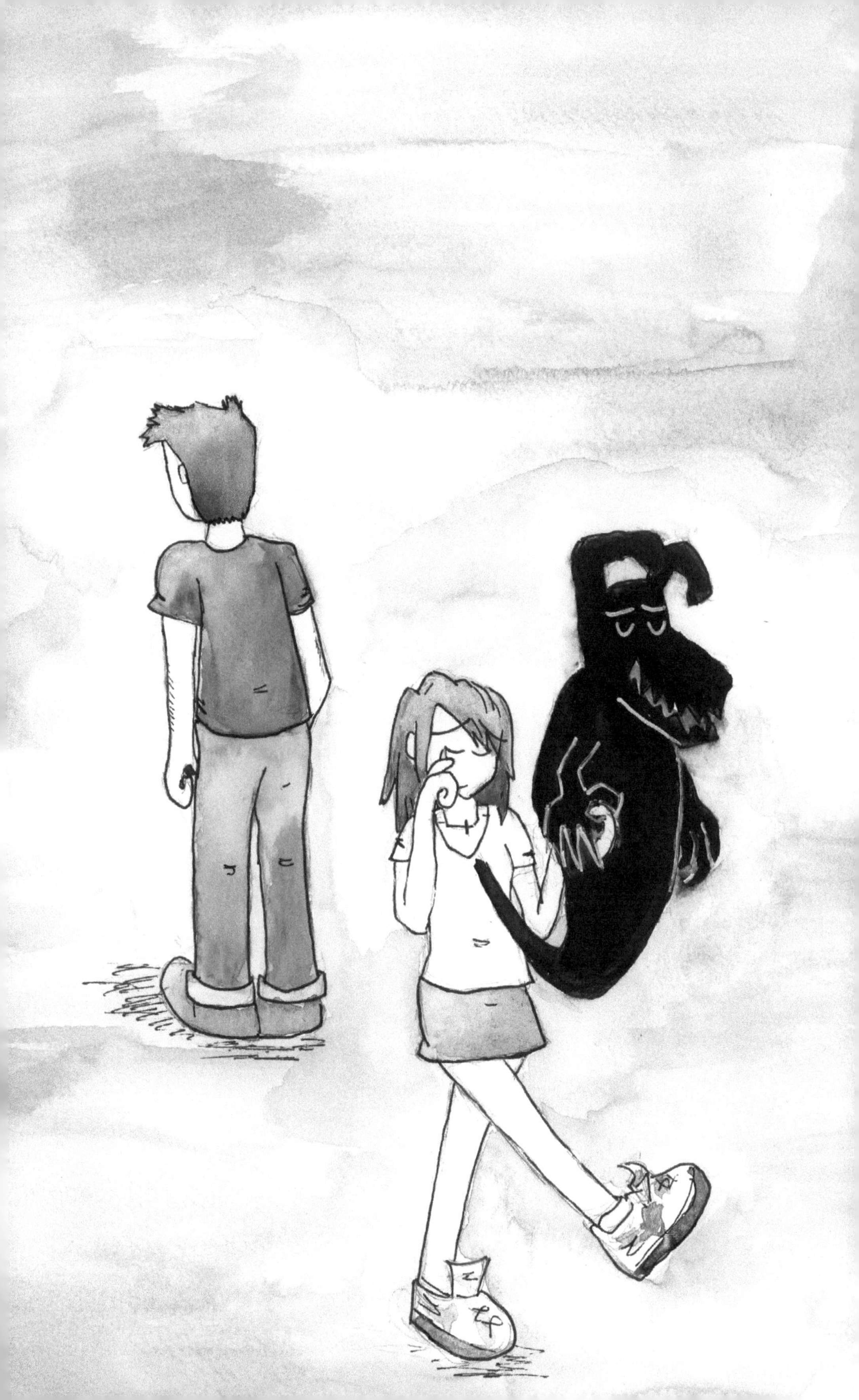

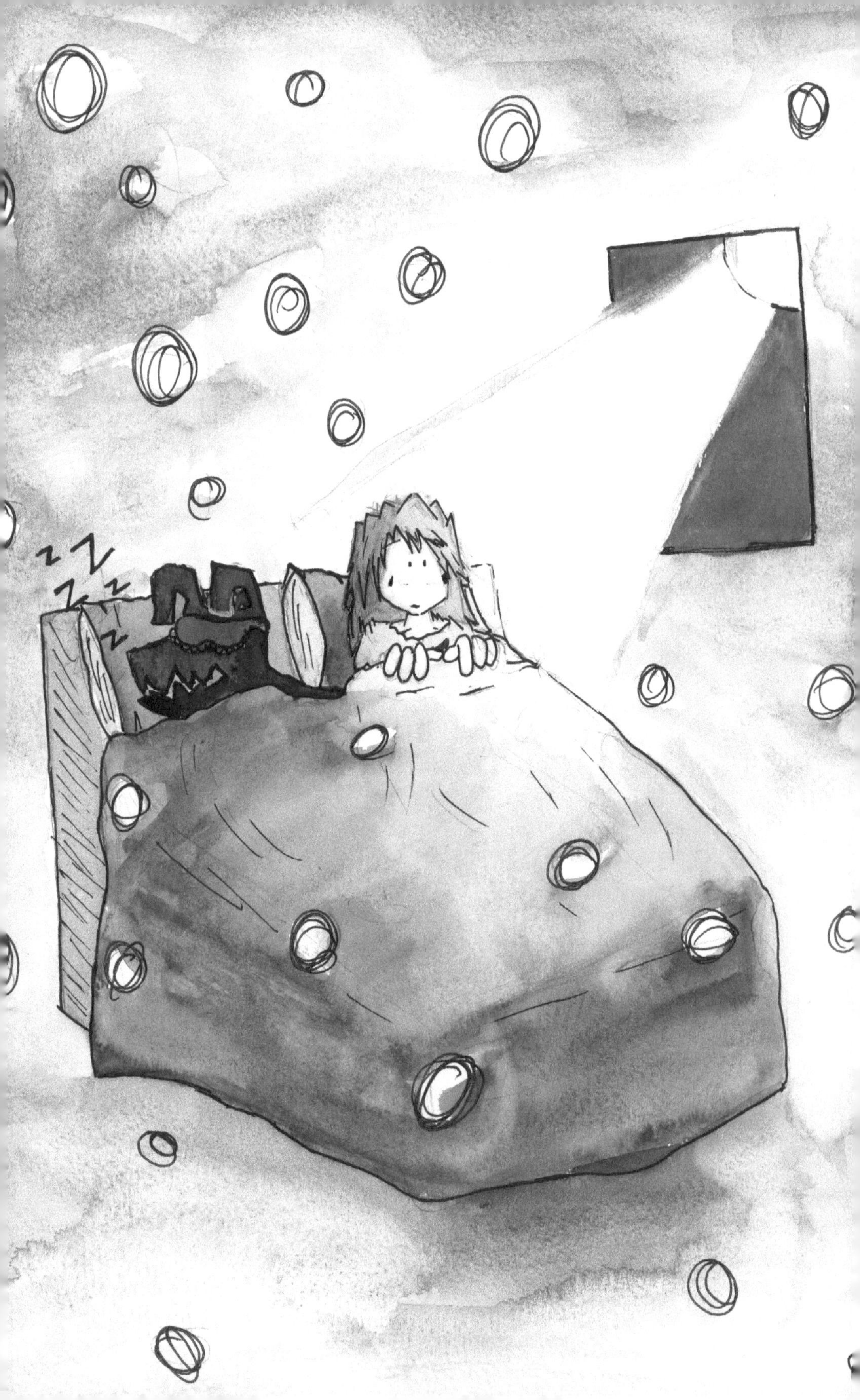

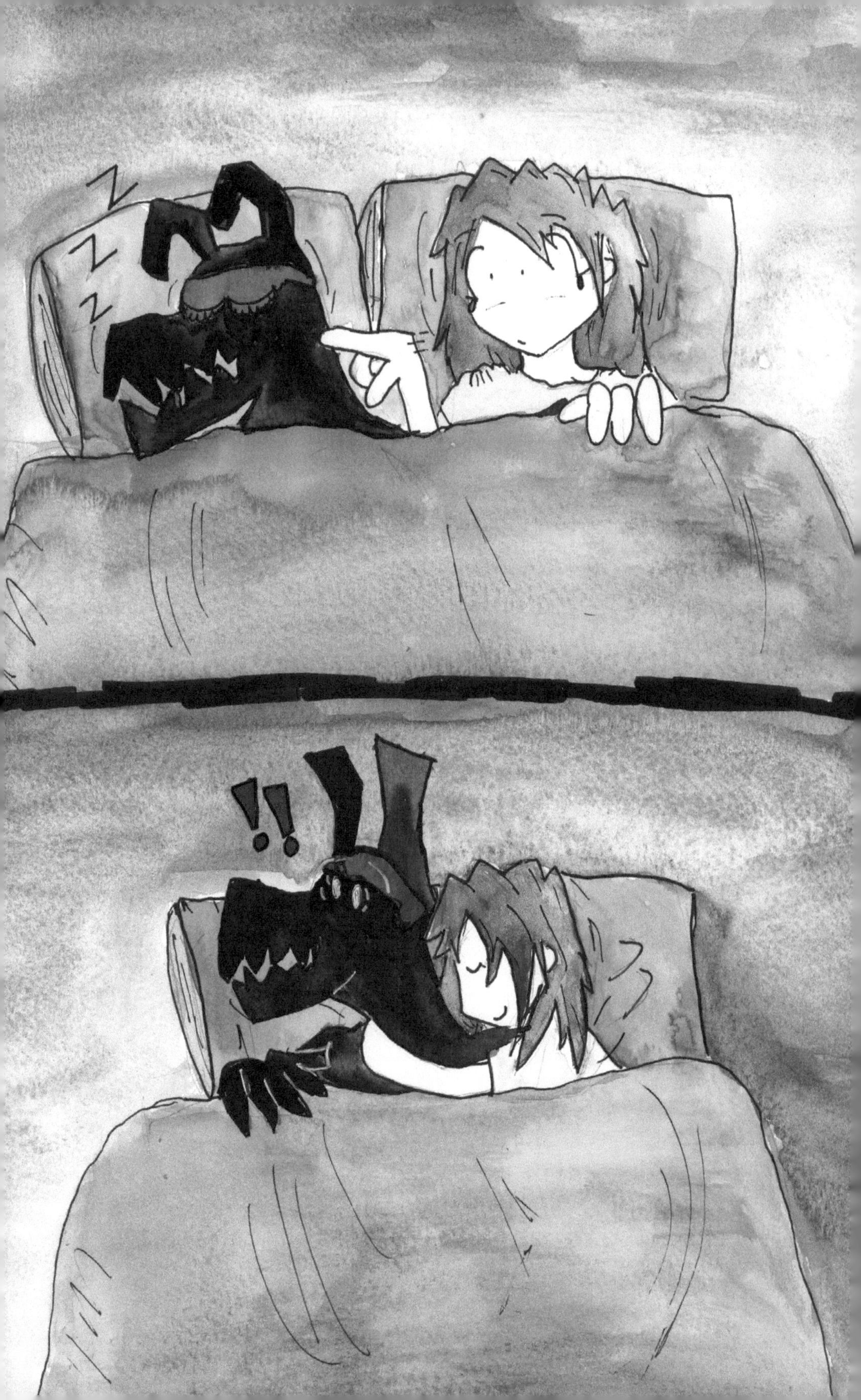
ZZZZ
!!

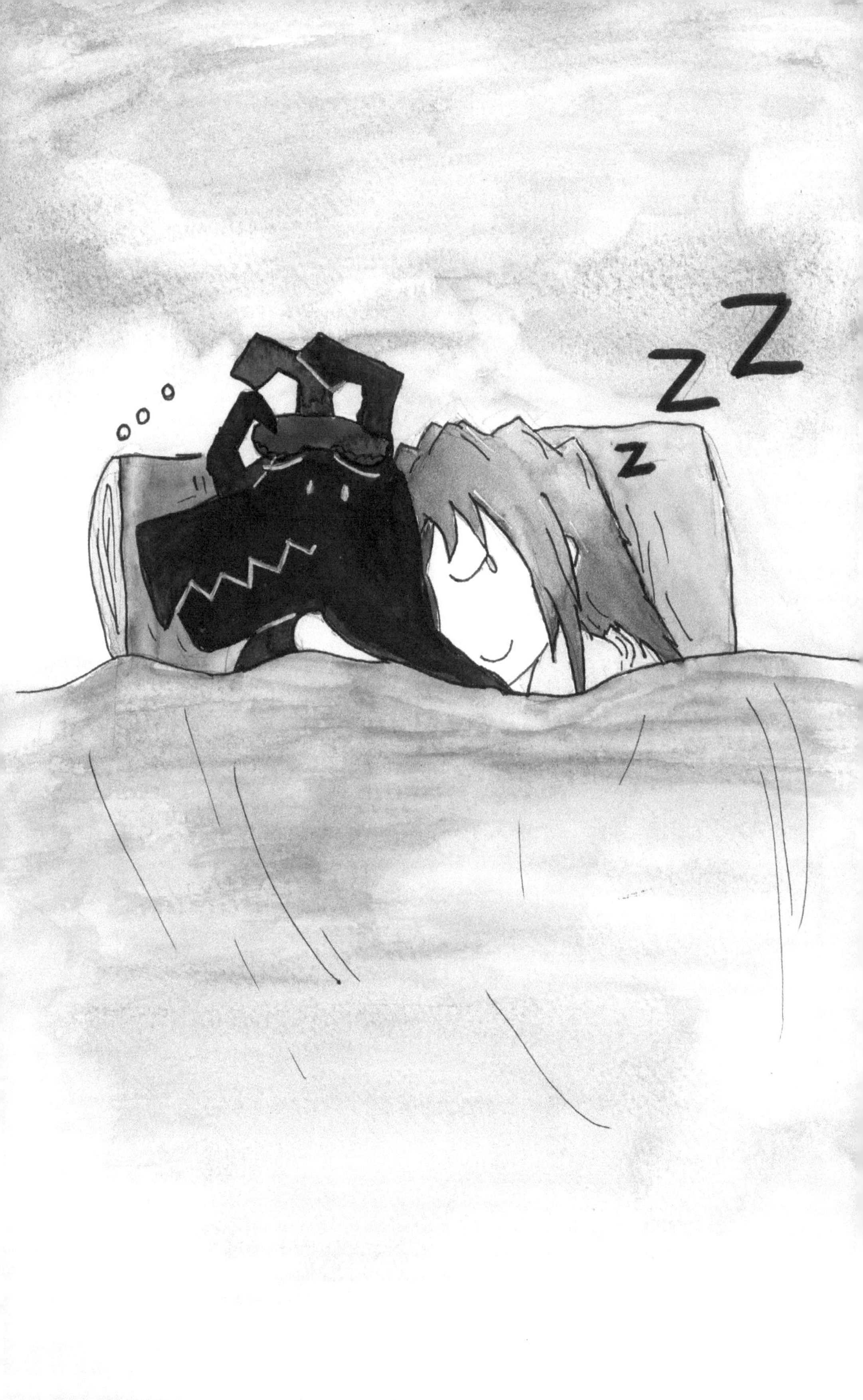
z Z Z

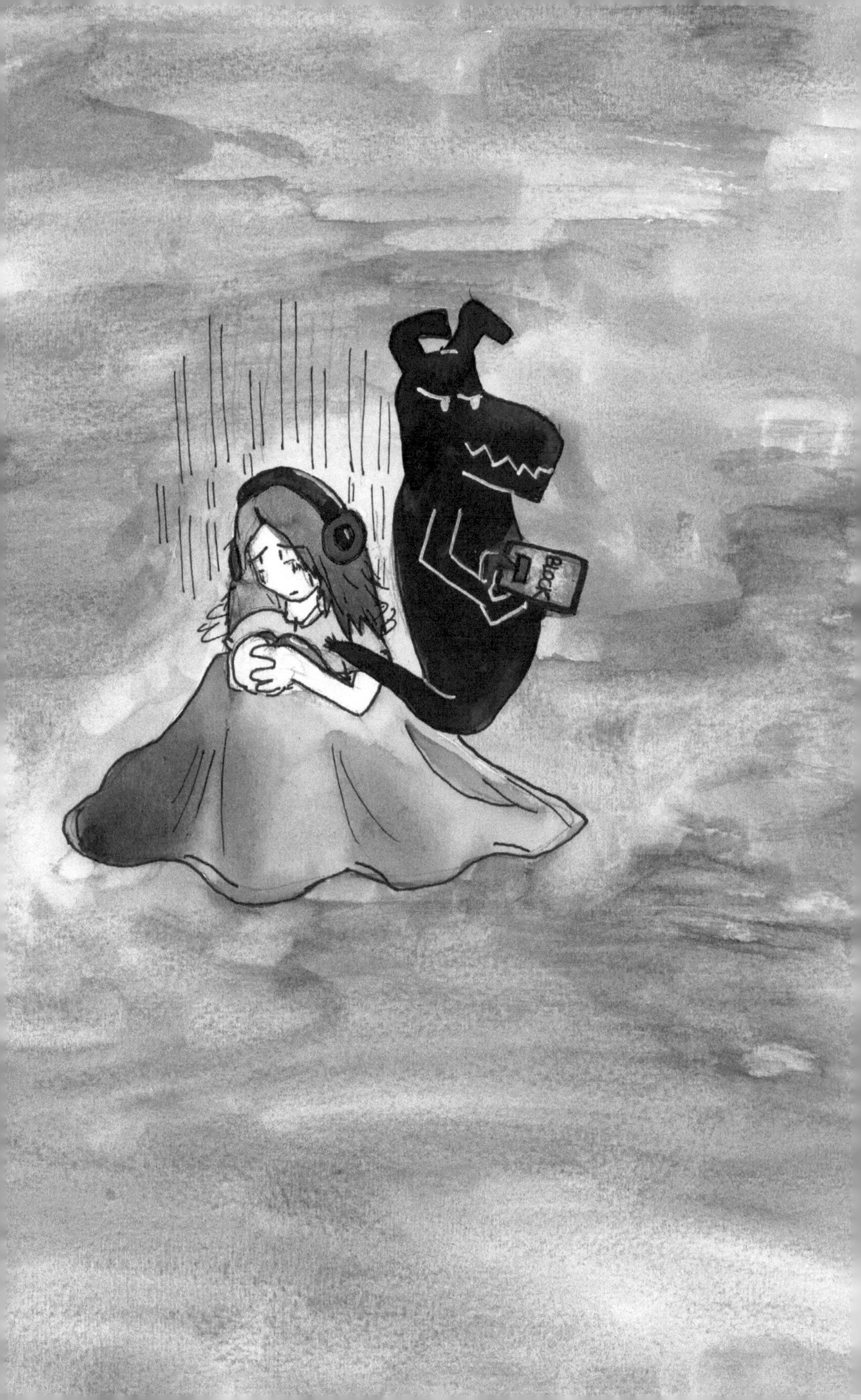
BLOCK

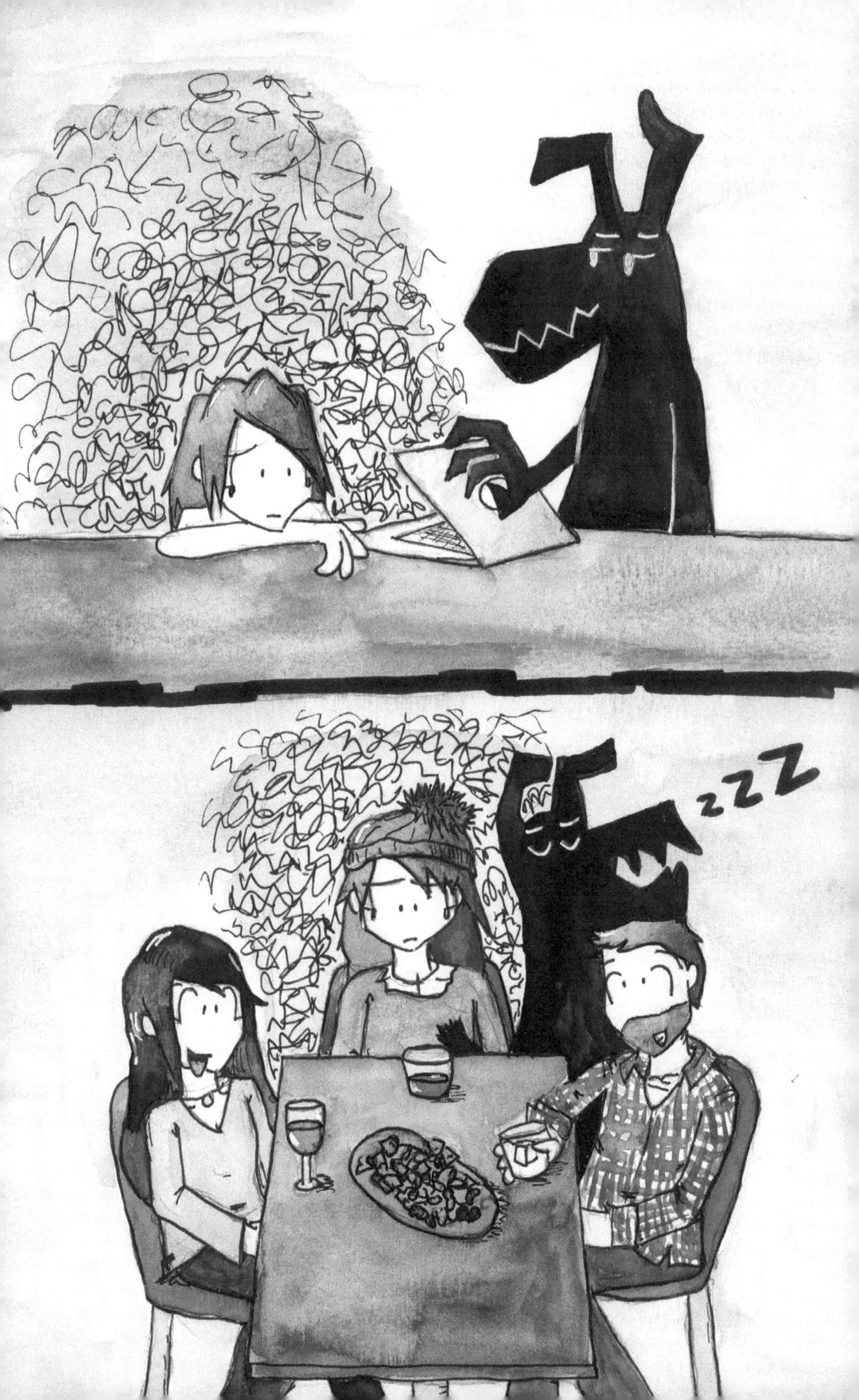
zzZ

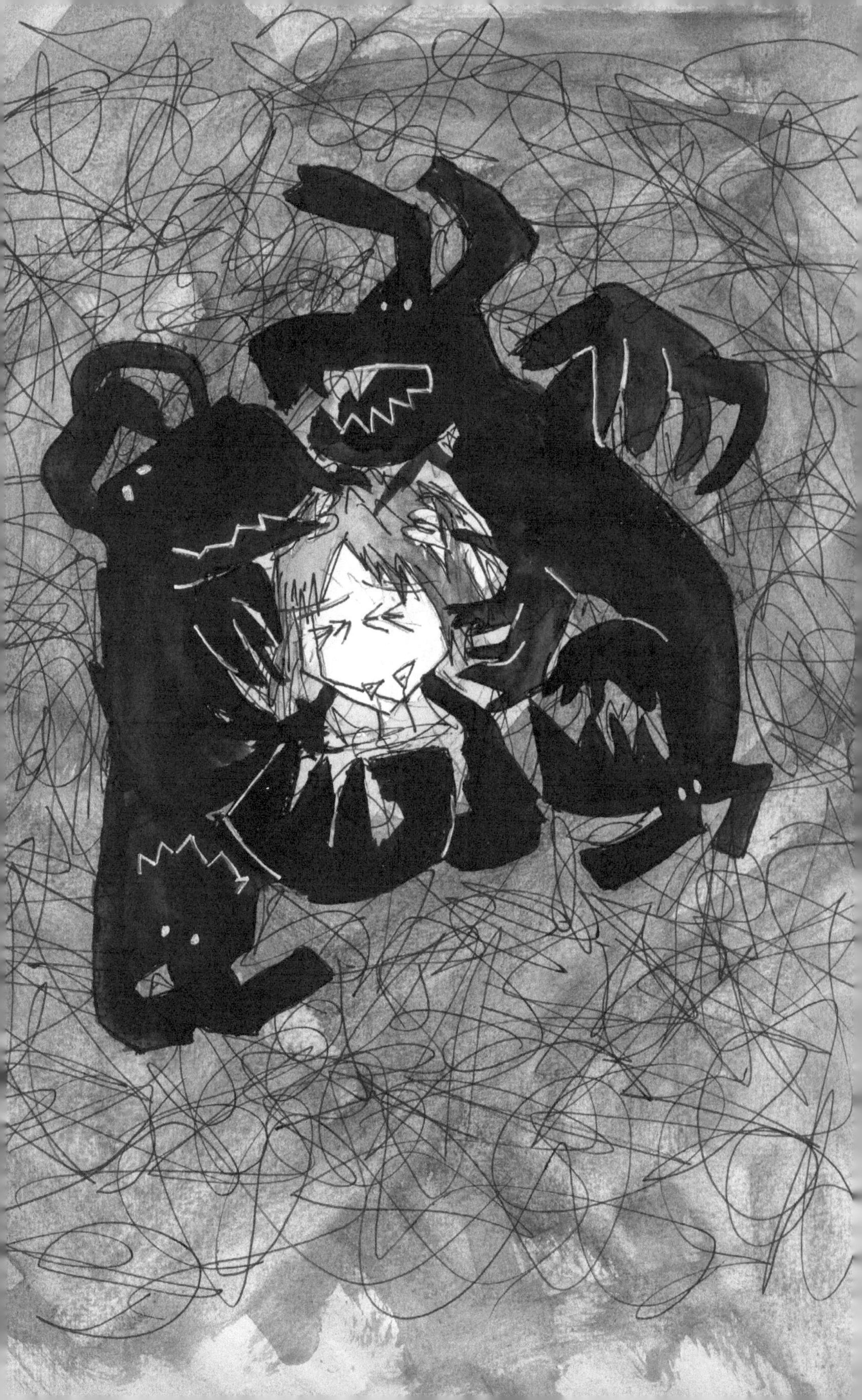

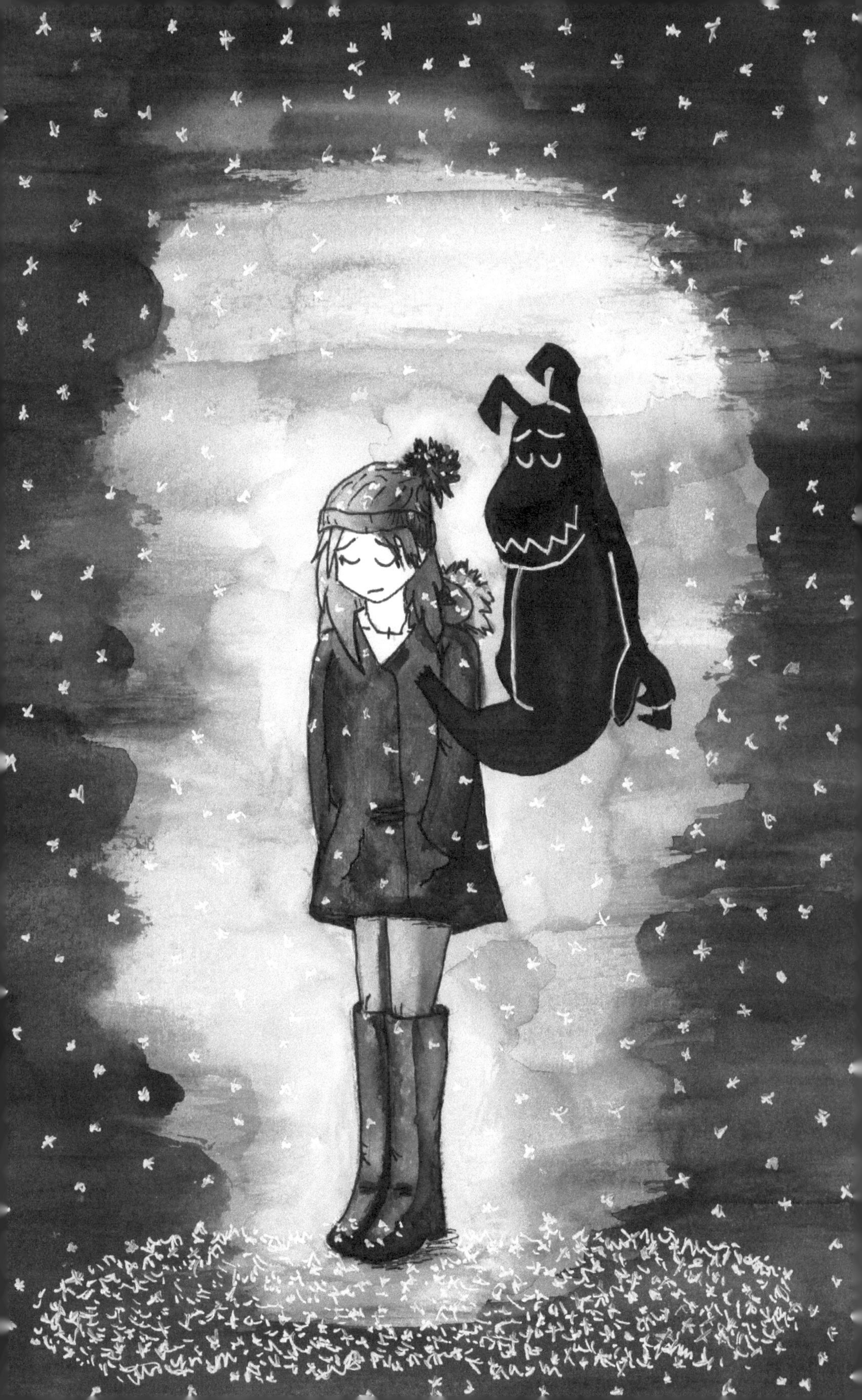

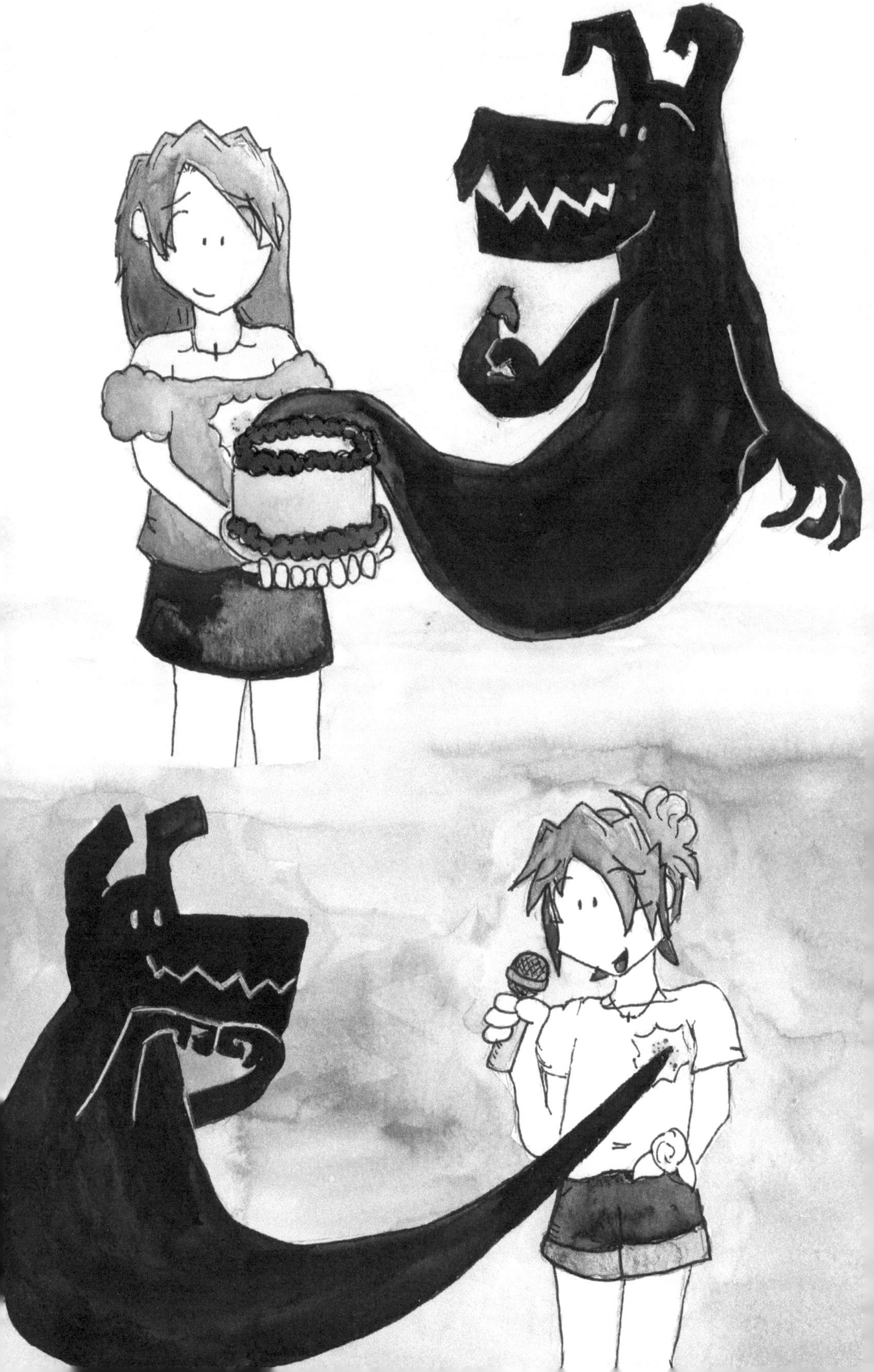

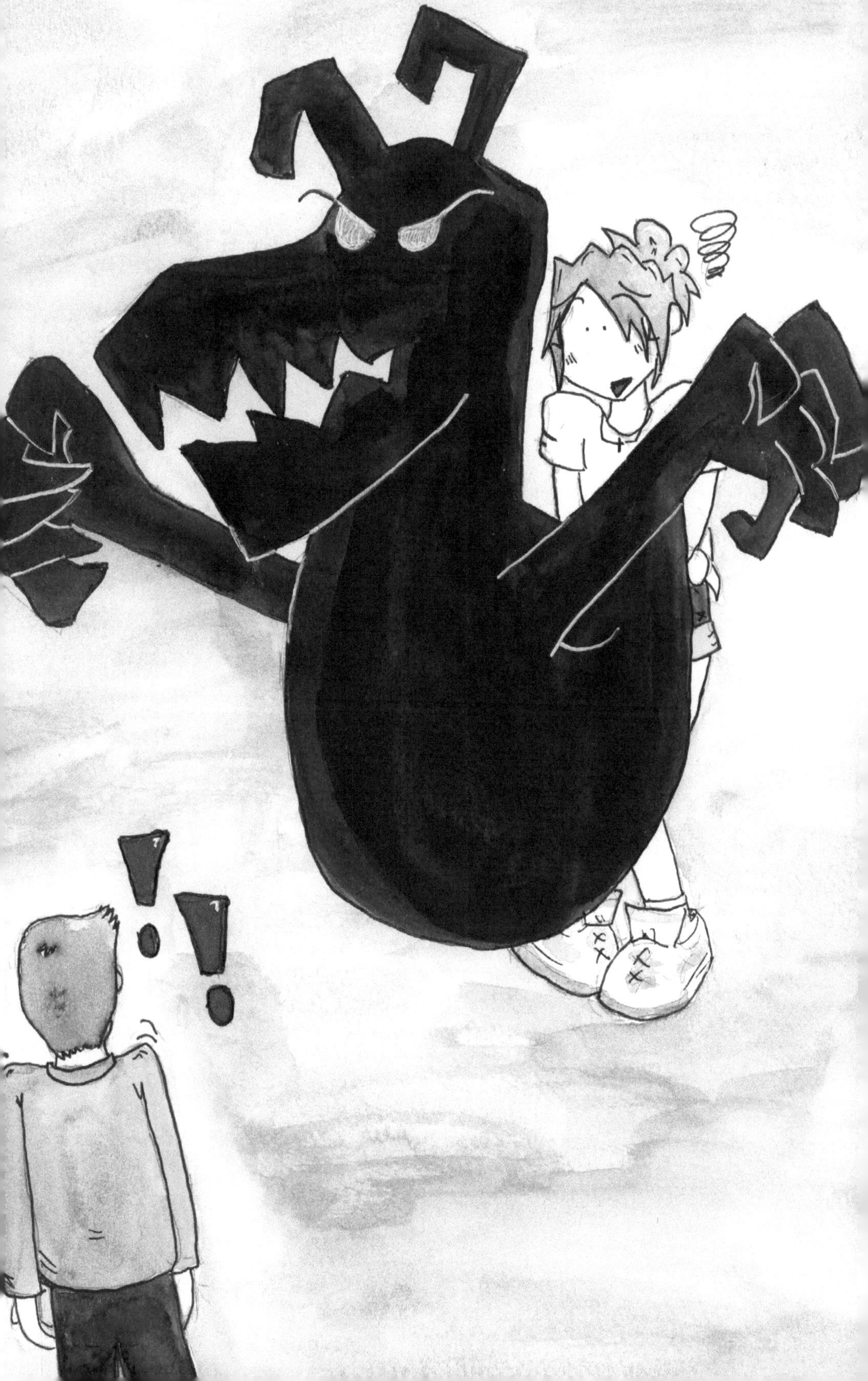

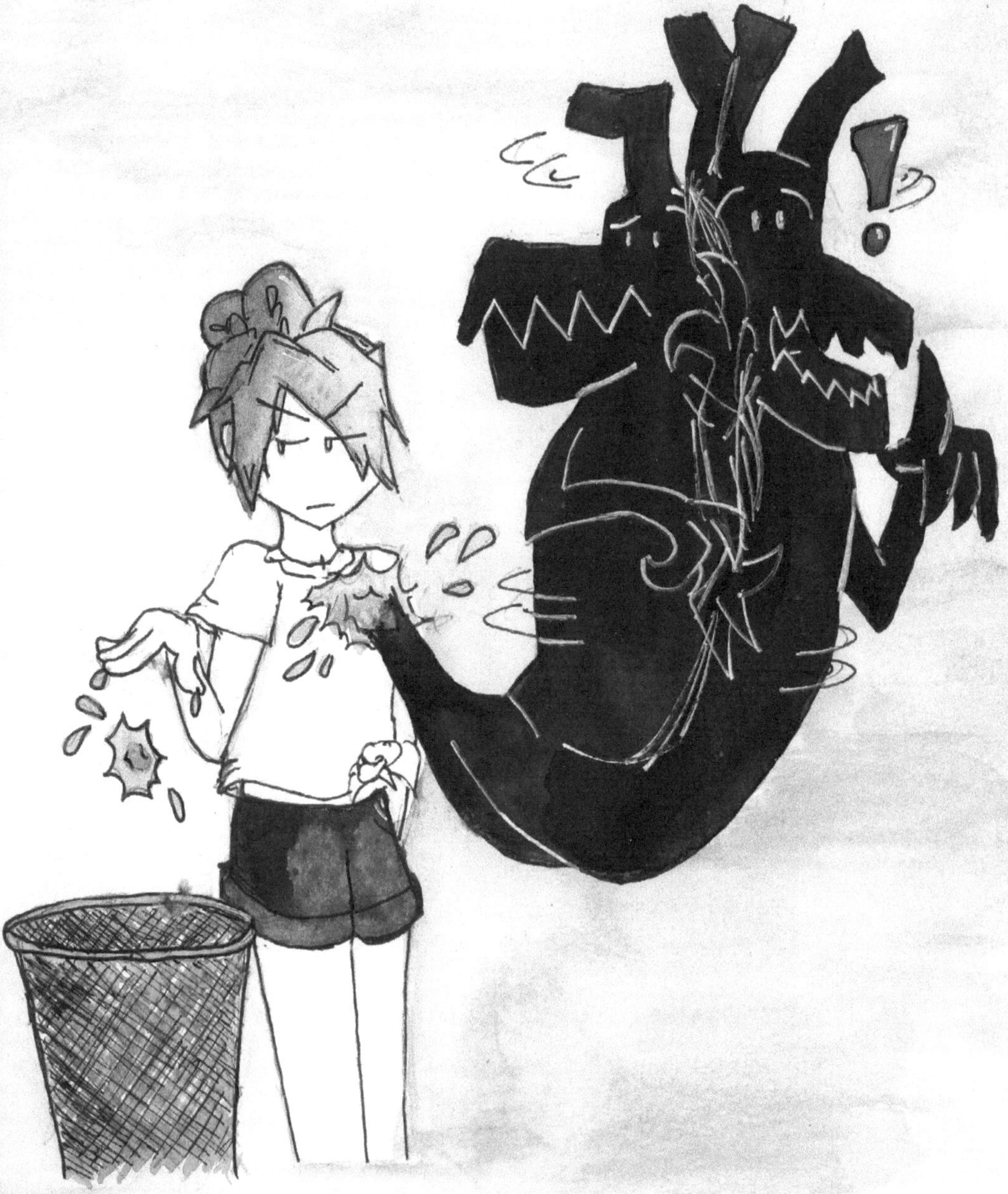

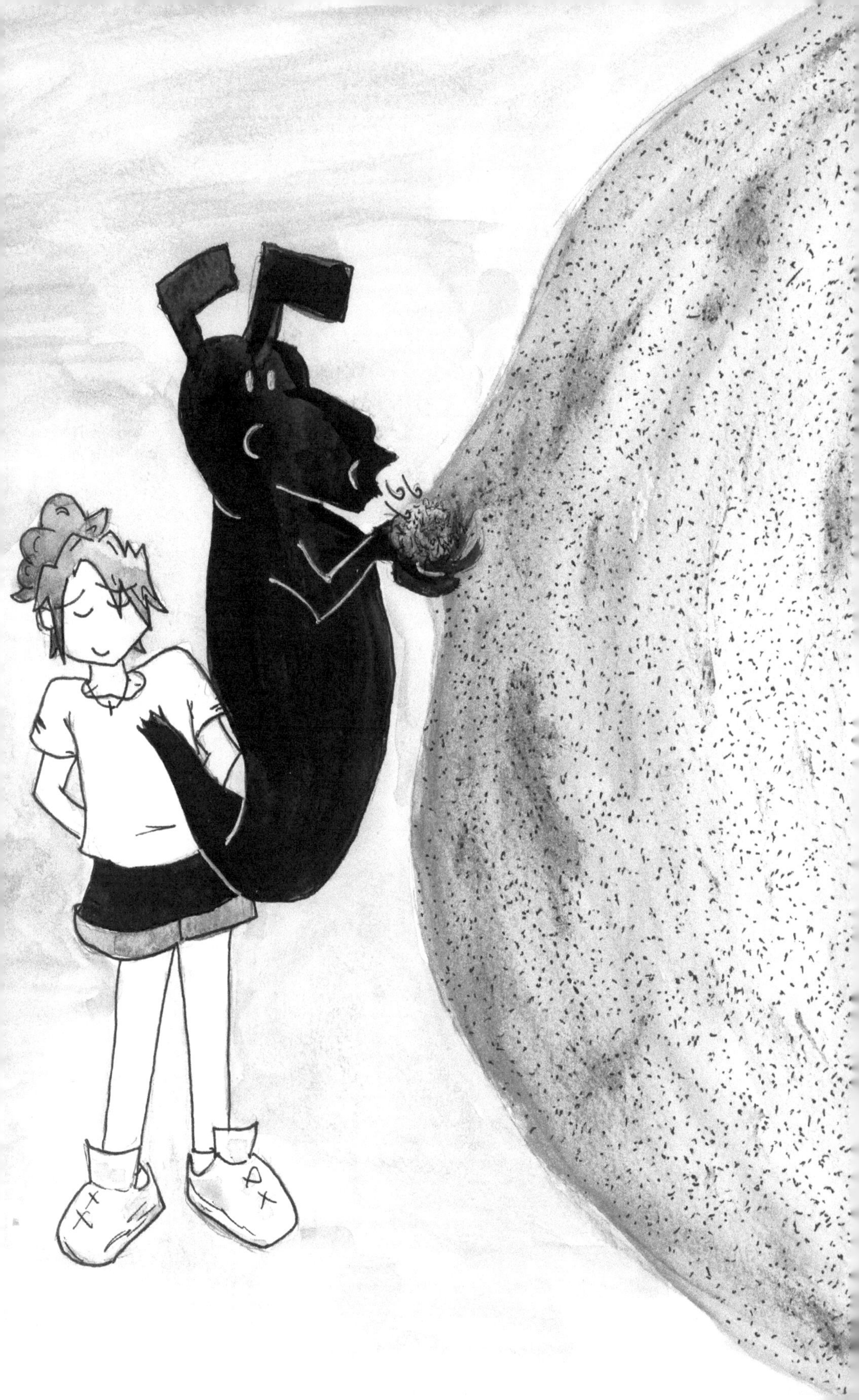

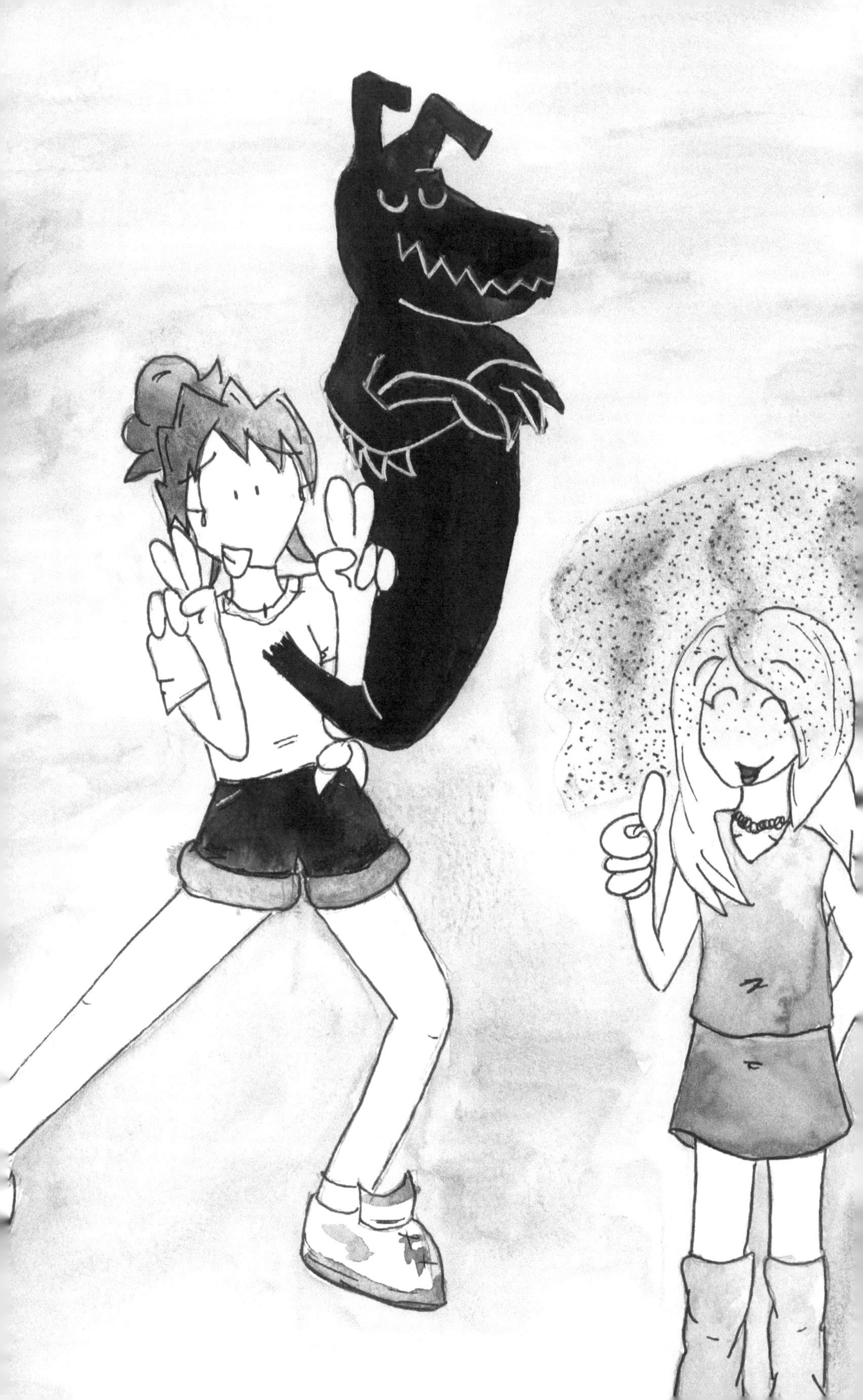

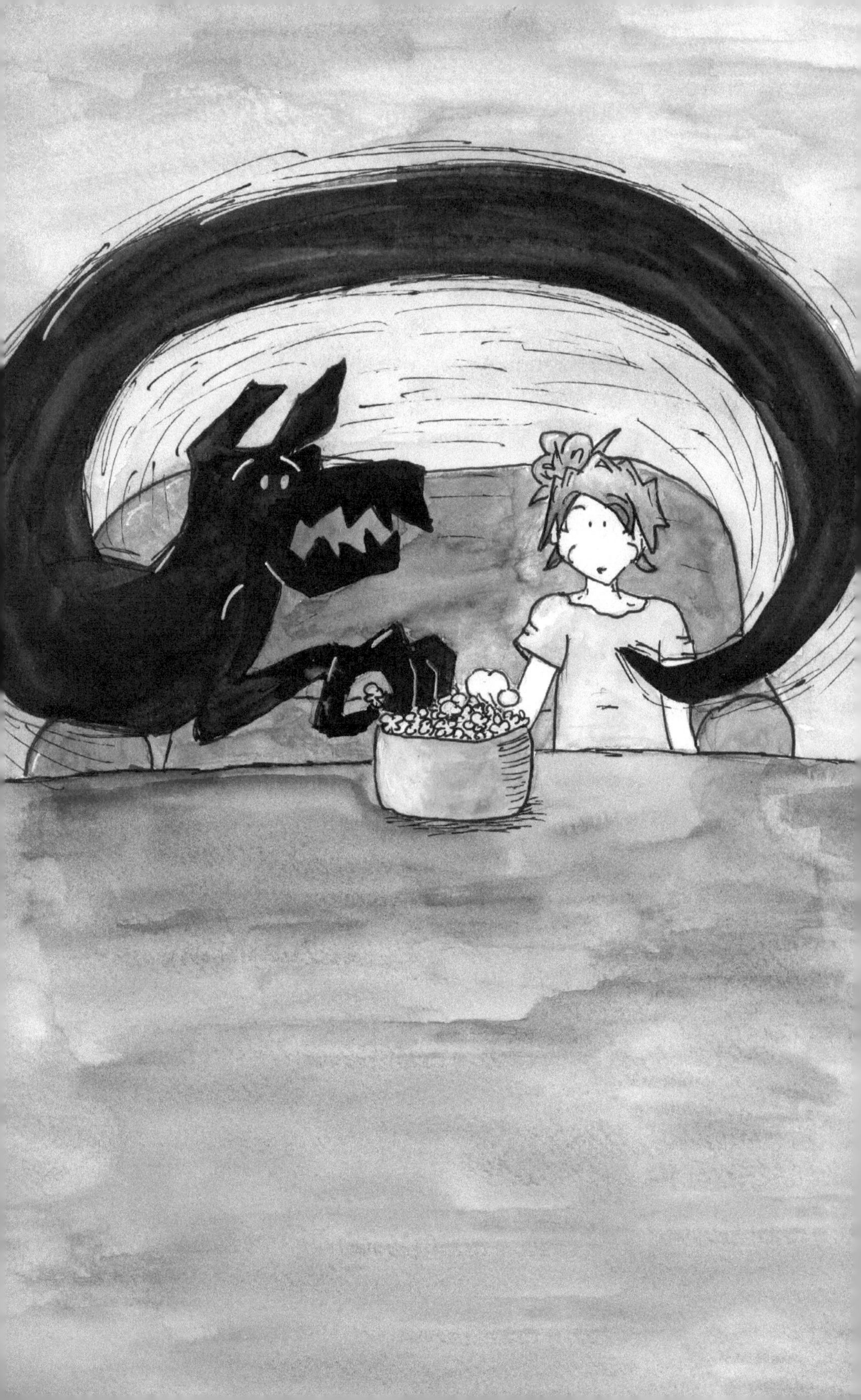

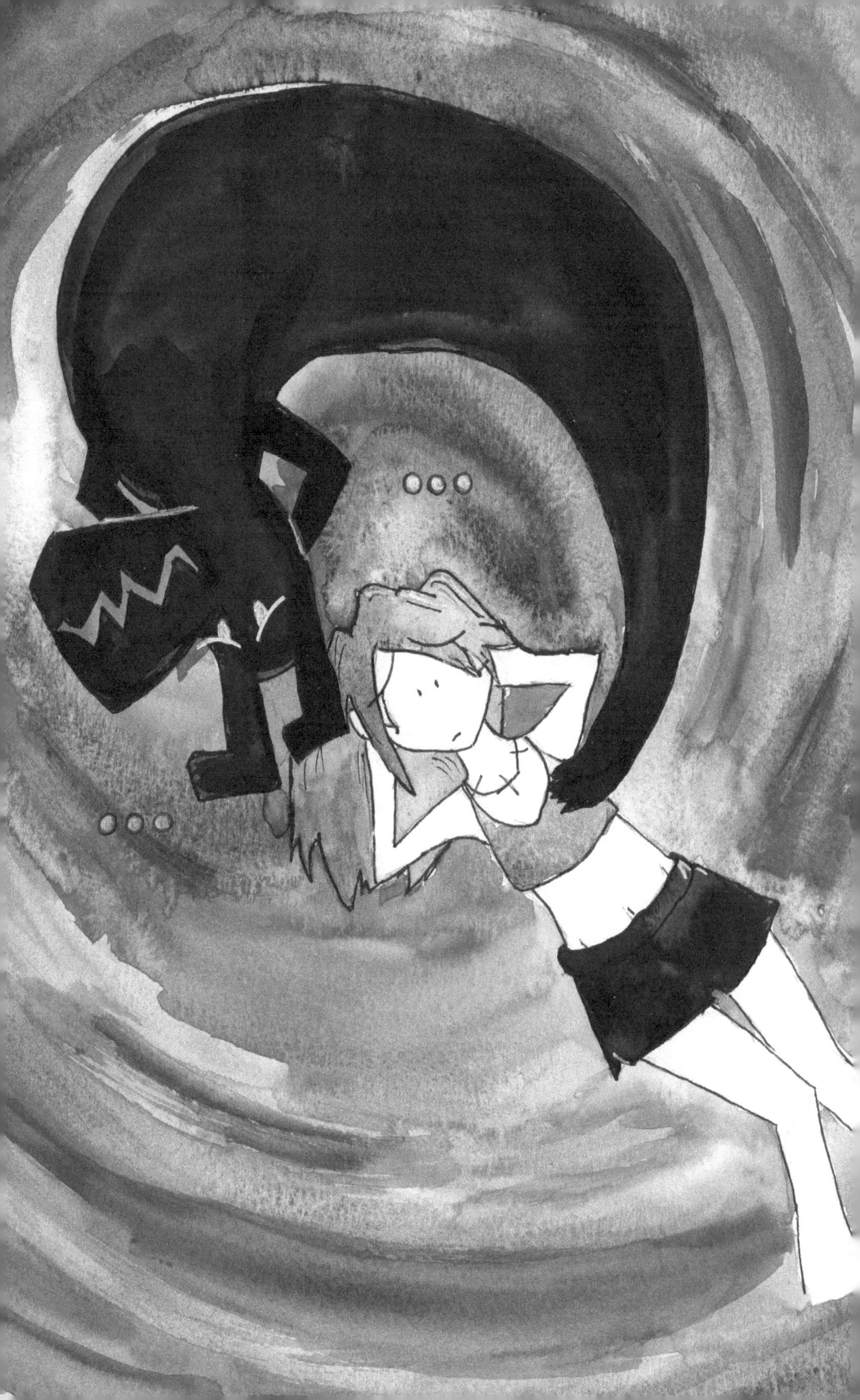

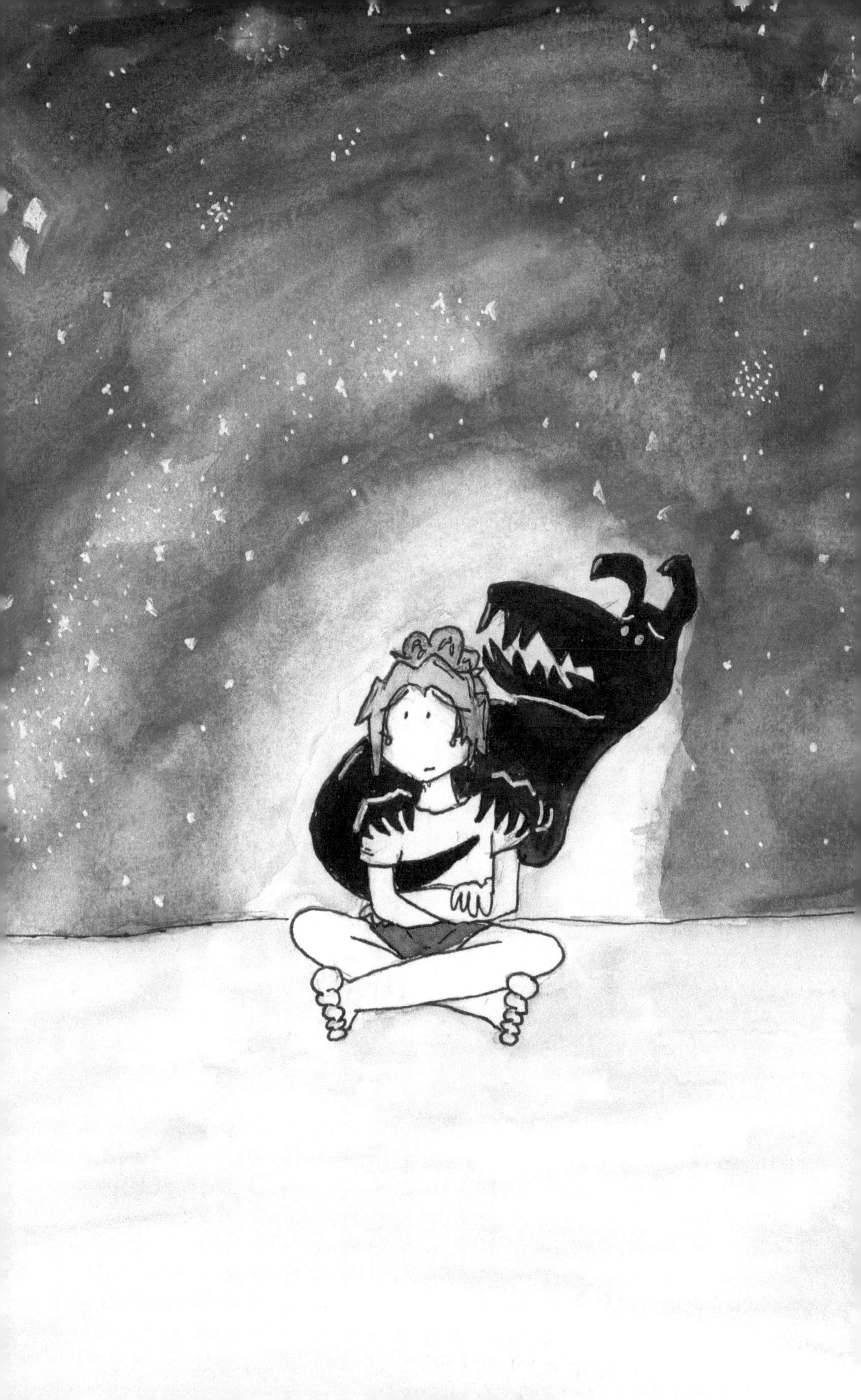

CPSIA information can be obtained
at www.ICGtesting.com
Printed in the USA
BVHW021919100222
628653BV00006B/52